So you really want to learn

Latin
Puzzles

BOOK 1

Julian Morgan

Series Editor: Nicholas Oulton

www.galorepark.co.uk

GALORE PARK

Published by Galore Park Publishing Ltd
19/21 Sayers Lane, Tenterden, Kent TN30 6BW

www.galorepark.co.uk

Text copyright © Julian Morgan 2006
Illustrations copyright Galore Park 2006

The right of Julian Morgan to be identified as the author of this Work has been
asserted by him in accordance with sections 77 and 78 of the Copyright,
Designs and Patents Act 1988.

Typography by Qué, Kent
Cover illustration by Ian Douglass

Printed and bound by CPI, Antony Rowe, Chippenham

ISBN-13 978 1 905735 05 1
ISBN-10 1 905735 05 7

First published 2006

Available in the So you really want to learn series
English
French
History
Latin
Maths
Science
Spanish

Latin may seem old fashioned to some people but in fact this ancient language is often incredibly useful in the modern world. Latin words are used in many European languages and in many modern environments such as the computing industry and the scientific community. The best reason to learn Latin, however, is that it can be great fun to do so: this book may help you to understand this point.

This collection of puzzles has been created using vocabulary from Level 1 of the Common Entrance Latin syllabus, to provide practice and entertainment for students working towards this examination. Also included are words and names from the non-linguistic section of the syllabus (e.g. the names of gods and goddesses) with which pupils should be familiar.

This book falls into two parts. In Part One (puzzles 1 to 25), hardly any inflections (changing word endings) are used, whereas in Part Two (puzzles 26 to 50) inflections are used to fit in with the grammatical content of the Level 1 syllabus: users can find a list of all the words used at the back of this book (page 58).

As you work your way through the exercises, expect them to get more difficult. For those of you who get really stuck, the solutions can be found at the back (pages 50 to 57)!

Julian Morgan

1   Mini crossword

In this crossword, the clues are in Latin but the answers must be in English. If you need help, you can use the Latin to English word list at the back of the book.

ACROSS
4   ostendo (1,4)
5   septimus (7)
7   numquam (5)

DOWN
1   video (1,3)
2   tamen (7)
3   altus (4)
5   navigo (4)
6   deinde (4)

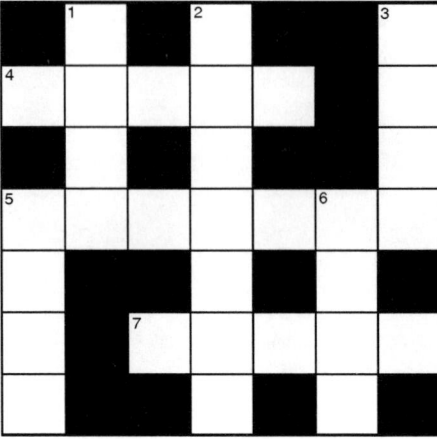

Note: Where a verb is given as a clue, such as maneo (= I remain), the word 'I' will sometimes, but not always, appear in the answer.

2   Mini Latin crossword

In this crossword, the clues are in English but the answers are in Latin! If you need help, you can use the English to Latin word list at the back of the book.

ACROSS
4   Roman (7)
5   Maid-servant (7)
6   I hurry (7)

DOWN
1   I give (2)
2   Arrow (7)
3   You (sing.) (2)
7   And (2)
8   Question mark? (2)

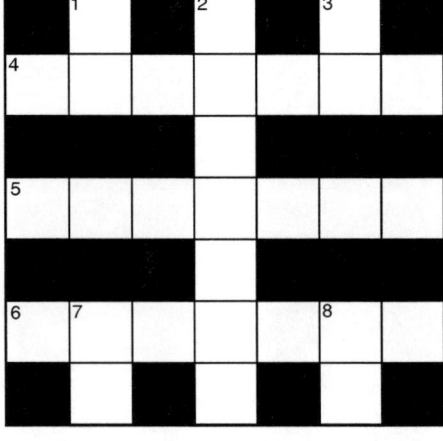

3   A top man

Fill in the words going across and then you can read the word which goes down on the left hand side of the grid to discover a top Roman. The English to Latin word list at the end should help you find the right answers, if you get stuck.

CLUES
1   I rule
2   Eight
3   My
4   Wave
5   I play
6   One
7   Their (own)

1			
2			
3			
4			
5			
6			
7			

The top man is: __ __ __ __ __ __ __

4   Keep smiling

In this crossword, all but one of the answers have been taken out and printed below. Your job is to fit all the other words back into the grid, and then write the clues! Don't forget to add the length of the answers in brackets.

OCTO
UNUS
SCUTUM
CAELUM
DOMINUS
~~ET RIDEO~~

ACROSS

3 ....

5 And I laugh (2,5)

6 ....

DOWN

I ....

2 ....

4 ....

5 Why not?

Look carefully at the grid below. The object of the puzzle is to find out which letter of the alphabet is represented by each of the 15 numbers used. You are given two words to start you off, so you can begin by entering any letters from this word wherever they appear in the grid. Each word you make should be in good Latin (you can check the Latin to English word list at the end if you need to). As you decode each letter, write it in the 'Letters deciphered' table and cross it off in the 'Letters used' table.

Letters deciphered:

1 C	2	3	4 N	5 U	6	7	8 O	9	10	11 R	12	13
14	15											

Letters used:

A	B	C	D	E	~~F~~	~~G~~	~~H~~	I	~~J~~	K	~~L~~	M
N	O	~~P~~	~~Q~~	R	S	T	U	V	~~W~~	X	~~Y~~	~~Z~~

6   At home

See how many of the words listed below you can find. They may be written across or down, or even diagonally. Oh yes, they could also be written backwards!

ATRIUM	FILIUS
COMPLUVIUM	HORTUS
CULINA	IANUA
DOMUS	IMPLUVIUM
FAUCES	MAGISTER
FILIA	MATER
PATER	TRICLINIUM
PERISTYLIUM	VILLA
TABLINUM	VIA

C	M	U	I	L	Y	T	S	I	R	E	P
O	U	L	R	O	I	D	F	S	B	A	T
M	S	L	A	T	R	D	U	A	T	L	T
P	R	F	I	B	T	I	S	U	I	L	R
L	A	I	L	N	L	S	I	N	L	I	S
U	I	T	I	I	A	T	B	A	I	V	U
V	P	M	R	H	A	T	R	I	U	M	M
I	M	A	P	I	O	R	L	T	S	T	O
U	O	I	T	L	C	R	E	D	I	T	D
M	D	R	L	E	U	L	T	T	P	F	A
D	P	T	R	I	R	V	I	U	A	B	I
S	E	C	U	A	F	D	I	N	S	M	L
M	A	G	I	S	T	E	R	U	I	R	I
F	T	I	P	T	Y	N	I	U	M	U	F
T	A	B	L	I	N	U	M	I	D	S	M

7 Sudoku

You probably know how Sudoku works. All you have to do is to place numbers one to nine in each vertical and horizontal line, and make sure that each number appears only once in each of the nine 3x3 squares. The difference here is that this is Roman Sudoku! Use the Roman numbers as below.

Roman numbers:

1	2	3	4	5	6	7	8	9
I	II	III	IV	V	VI	VII	VIII	IX

Good luck – feliciter!

	V	VI	IV		VIII	I		
VII			IX		V			II
		IV	VI				V	III
	III		VIII					IX
V	II						VI	VIII
VIII					VII		II	
I	IX				III	VII		
III			VII		IX			VI
		II	I		IV	IX	III	

8   Crossword

In this crossword, the clues are in Latin but the answers are all in English. If you need help, you can use the Latin to English word list at the back of the book.

ACROSS
5   pulcher (9)
8   verbum (4)
9   mox (4)
13   nuntius (9)

DOWN
1   decem (3)
2   aedifico (5)
3   sex (3)
4   sed (3)
6   duo (3)
7   unus (3)
9   sto (5)
10   video (3)
11   rogo (3)
12   novus (3)

Note: Where a verb is given as a clue, such as maneo (= I remain), the word 'I' will sometimes, but not always, appear in the answer.

9 Find the monster!

A monster is on the loose but if you know his name, you will be able to finish him off. Fill in the grid below and work out who he is by putting together the letters from the shaded boxes. Use the English to Latin word list at the back, if you need help.

ACROSS
1 I carry (5)
4 I depart (7)
9 Greatly (9)
10 To (2)
12 Down from (2)
13 Who (4)
14 For a long time (3)
15 Wall (5)
18 What (4)
19 Here (3)
21 Arrow (7)
24 I sing (5)
25 Three (4)
26 Through (3)
27 Anger (3)
28 Their (4)
29 Not (3)
30 I decide (9)

DOWN
2 I show (7)
3 Temple (7)
5 Slave (6)
6 Goddess (3)
7 I (3)
8 Ally (6)
11 Then (6)
16 I answer (9)
17 Safe (5)
18 Fourth (7)
20 Against (6)
22 Sword (7)
23 Again (6)
24 I desire (5)

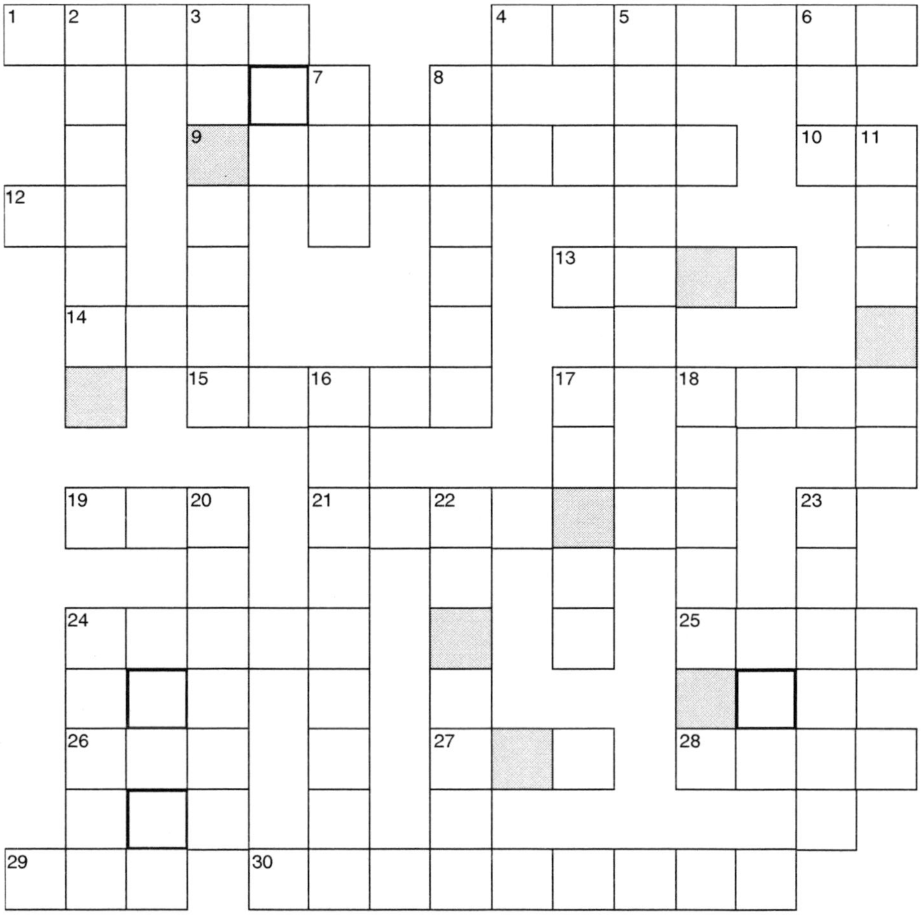

The monster's name is: __ __ __ __ __ __ __ __

10 Latin crossword

In this crossword, the clues are in English, but the answers are all in Latin. If you need help you can use the English to Latin word list at the back of the book.

ACROSS
1   Water (4)
2   Because (4)
5   Horse (5)
6   I depart (7)
9   Poet (5)
10 Eight (4)
11 I play (4)

DOWN
1   Field (4)
3   I say (4)
4   Beautiful (7)
7   I put (4)
8   I read (4)

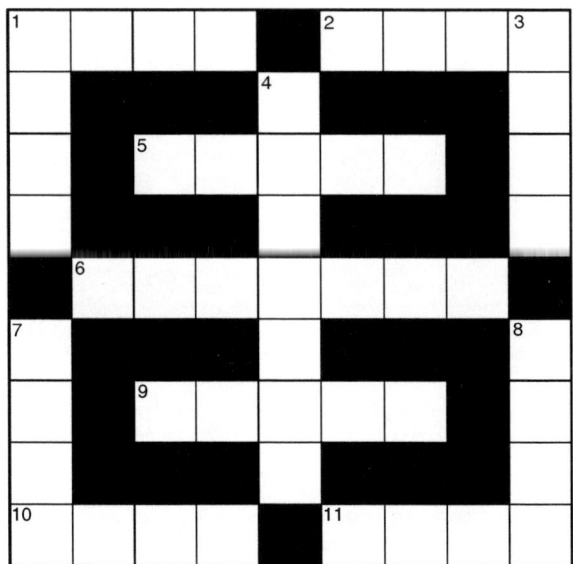

11 Cryptic Latin crossword

The answers to this mind-bender are all in Latin. You may need to use the word lists at the back for help.

ACROSS

1   Aim is skewed now (3)
3   Rat go back inside, he asks (5)
5   What reason for me to do it? (3,3)
6   We get two compass points around a circle (3)
7   Not anonymous within (3)
9   So I turn without the North after a not so quiet pig (6)
10 Confusion at holy races (5)
11 My existence counts (3)

DOWN

2   Murmur usefully inside construction (5)
3   Muddled goer – I'm in charge (4)
4   But thanks, chaps (5)
6   Sun back and on top, but not quite tenth (5)
7   Known to stun badly with nothing inside (5)
8   Makes you feel old in the countryside (4)

12 Arrow word

All the clues are on the grid. You can use the English to Latin word list at the back to help, if you want. The answers are all in Latin.

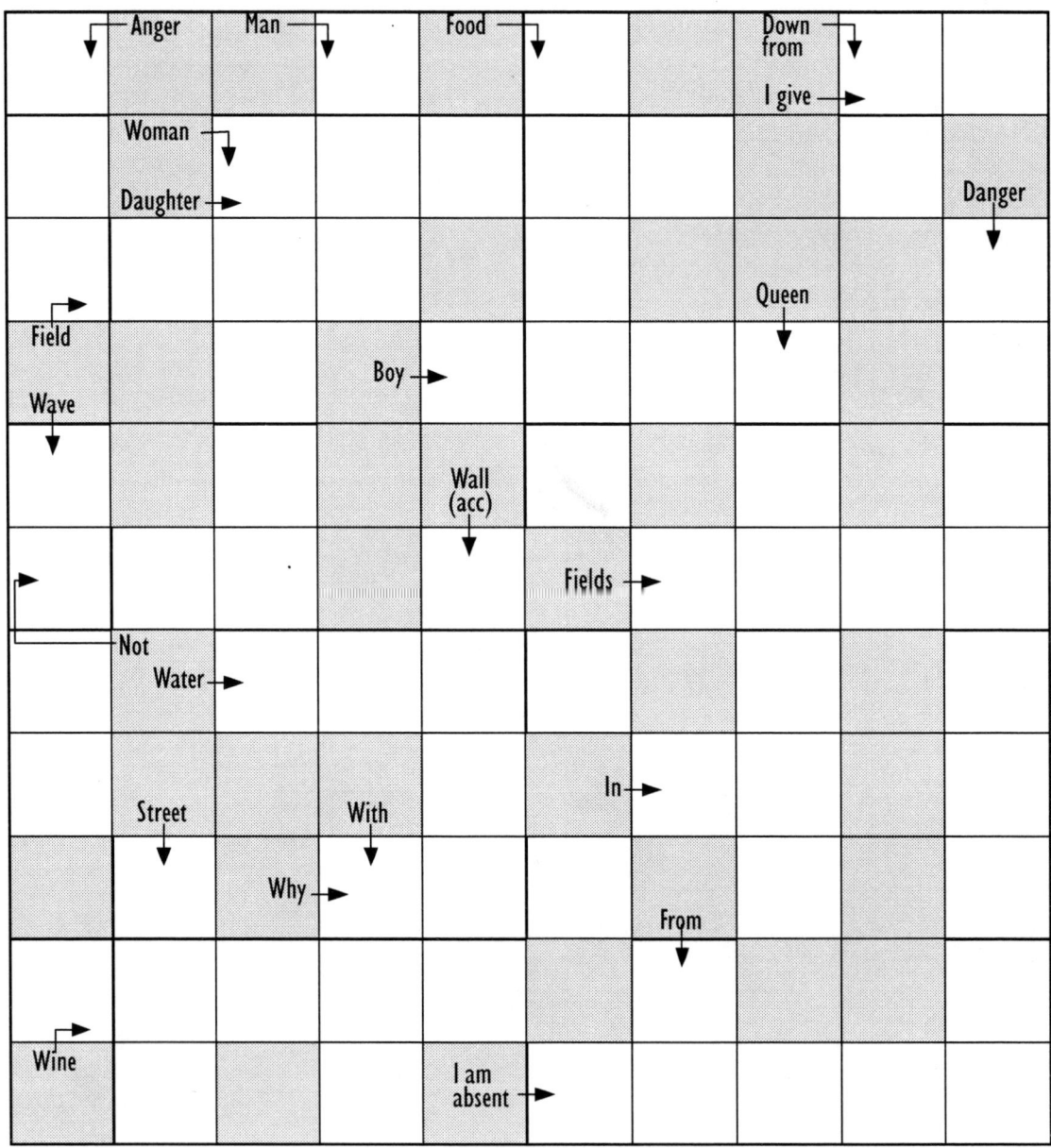

13 Room in the house

Fill in the words in Latin going across and then you will be able to read a word down through the middle of the grid and discover a part of a Roman house. Use the English to Latin word list at the back if you need help.

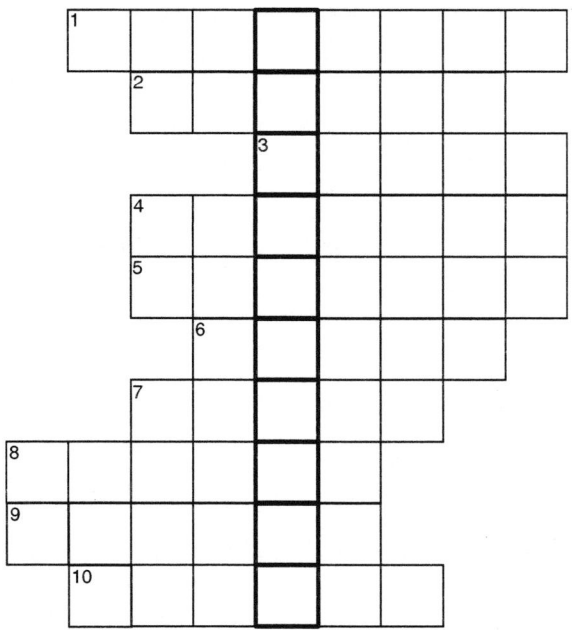

CLUES

1	Bravely (8)
2	Small (6)
3	I throw (5)
4	Money (7)
5	Strong (7)
6	Book (5)
7	I warn (5)
8	Native land (6)
9	Wind (6)
10	First (6)

The part of the house is: __ __ __ __ __ __ __ __ __

14 Fit the words

Try to fit all the Latin words into the grid below.

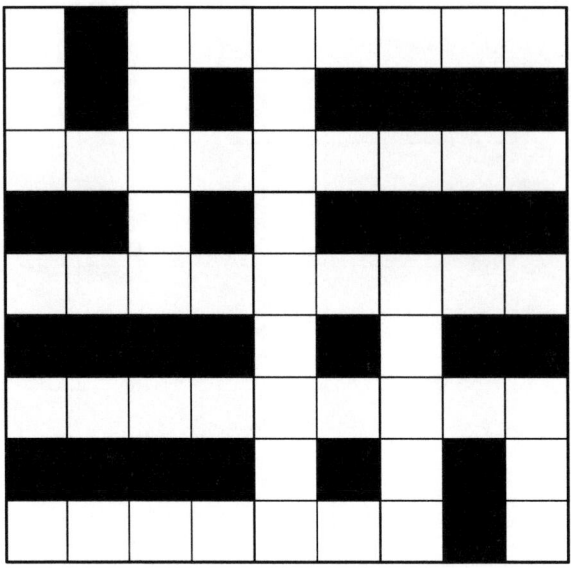

3 letters
MOX
NON

5 letters
DELEO
NOVUS

7 letters
DISCEDO
NUMQUAM

9 letters
MAGNOPERE
NAVIGO IBI
PER BELLUM
RESPONDEO

15 Latin crossword

In this crossword, the clues are in English but the answers are all in Latin. If you need help, you can use the English to Latin word list at the back of the book.

ACROSS
3   Farmer (8)
5   To (2)
6   Six (3)
7   My (4)
8   Down from (2)
9   Out of (2)
10   Eight (4)
11   I love (3)
13   In (2)
15   Battle (8)

DOWN
1   Three (4)
2   We (3)
3   I build (8)
4   Help (8)
7   Soon (3)
8   Two (3)
12   Once (4)
14   You (pl.) (3)

16 Crossword

In this crossword, the clues are in Latin but the answers are all in English. The Latin to English word list at the back of the book will help, if you need it.

ACROSS
1   meus magister (2,6)
5   magnus (3)
7   ager (5)
8   nos (2)
9   mox (3)
10   venio (4)
12   deinde (4)
13   aurum (4)
14   meus (2)
15   laetus (5)
16   iam (3)
18   deleo (1,7)

DOWN
2   sum? (2,1)
3   subito (8)
4   secundus (6)
6   bonus (4)
8   miser (8)
9   dormit (6)
11   oppidum (4)
17   ex (3)

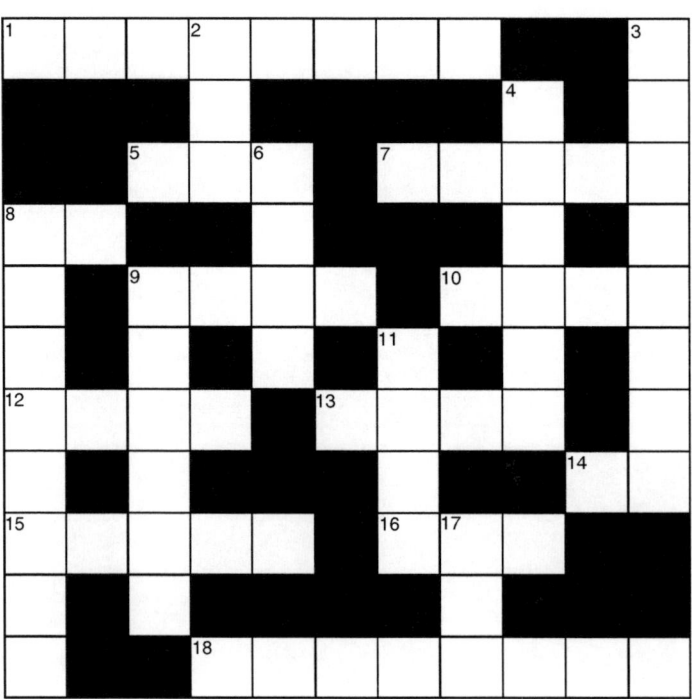

Note: Where a verb is given as a clue, such as maneo (= I remain), the word 'I' will sometime,s but not always, appear in the answer.

17 Missing mythology

Find the mythical characters from the stories of Perseus and Theseus in the grid below. They may be written across or down, or even diagonally. Oh yes, they could also be written backwards!

ACRISIUS	CENTAUR	MEDUSA	PLUTO
AEGEUS	DANAE	MINOS	POLYDECTES
AETHRA	GRAIAE	MINOTAUR	PROCRUSTES
AMAZONS	HERMES	PASIPHAE	SCYRON
ANDROMEDA	HIPPOLYTA	PERSEUS	SINIS
ARIADNE	LAPITHS	PHAEDRA	THESEUS
ATLAS	MEDEA	PITTHEUS	ZEUS

D	A	N	A	E	M	I	N	O	S	O	T	U	L	P
Z	A	D	S	T	P	N	E	N	P	S	S	H	P	O
G	S	U	E	Z	L	T	T	C	R	E	H	I	R	L
R	E	I	R	M	N	A	E	S	L	P	T	P	O	Y
A	R	S	N	Z	O	N	S	P	R	T	I	P	C	D
I	P	E	T	I	T	R	S	L	H	R	P	O	R	E
A	P	A	T	A	S	U	D	E	M	A	A	L	U	C
E	A	A	U	S	E	L	U	N	M	S	L	Y	S	T
T	R	R	S	S	A	S	E	H	A	R	P	T	T	E
H	U	P	E	I	S	C	Y	R	O	N	E	A	E	S
R	A	H	A	S	E	S	R	Z	H	G	N	H	S	U
A	T	S	T	N	G	I	R	I	P	M	Z	T	P	E
T	O	H	E	G	E	S	U	E	S	R	E	P	T	G
H	N	P	H	A	E	D	R	A	R	I	A	D	N	E
E	I	N	S	N	O	Z	A	M	A	R	U	R	E	A
S	M	G	P	E	A	H	P	I	S	A	P	S	E	A

18 Mini crossword

In this crossword, the clues are in Latin but the answers are in English. If you need help, you can use the Latin to English word list at the back of the book.

ACROSS
1   laudo (1,6)
4   venit (5)
6   numquam (5)
7   septimus (7)

DOWN
2   Romanus (5)
3   intro (5)
4   vocat (5)
5   septem (5)

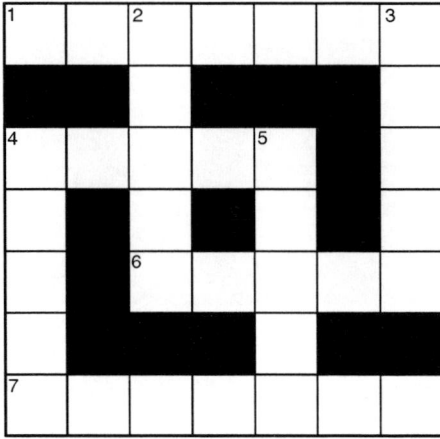

Note: Where a verb is given as a clue, such as maneo (= I remain), the word 'I' will sometimes, but not always, appear in the answer.

19 Mini Latin crossword

In this crossword, the clues are in English but the answers must be in Latin! If you need help, you can use the English to Latin word list at the back of the book.

ACROSS
1   Eighth (7)
3   Friend (6)
4   Much (6)
5   Roman (7)

DOWN
2   Maid-servant (7)

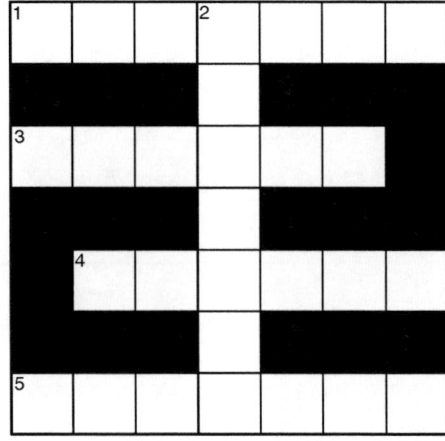

20 Good what?

Fill in the words going across and then you will uncover, going down the grid, a Latin expression which is commonly used in English. The English to Latin word list at the back will help you find the right answers if you get stuck. Don't forget to put the length of the answer in brackets.

CLUES
1   Greatly (9)
2   I move (5)
3   Spear (5)
4   At last (6)
5   Crowd (5)
6   Queen (6)
7   Island (6)
8   Often (5)

The Latin expression is: __ __ __ __   __ __ __ __ __

21 Where and why?

In this crossword, all but two of the answers have been taken out and printed below. Your job is to fit all the other words back into the grid, and then write the clues! Don't forget to put the length of the answer in brackets.

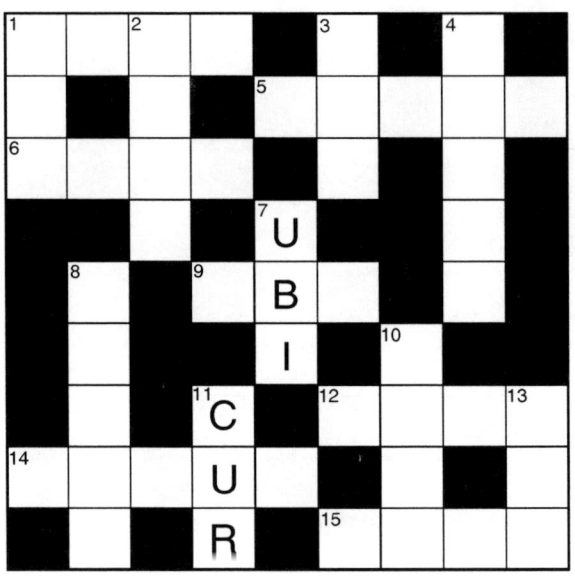

CUR	PER	PARO	ADSUM
EGO	UBI	REGO	CANTO
IAM	BENE	ROGO	ETIAM
IBI	NECO	VOCO	LAUDO

ACROSS

1 ....

5 ....

6 ....

9 ....

12 ....

14 ....

15 ....

DOWN

1 ....

2 ....

3 ....

4 ....

7 Where? (3)

8 ....

10 ....

11 Why? (3)

13 ....

22 A Roman mystery

Look carefully at the grid below. The object of the puzzle is to find out which letter of the alphabet is represented by each of the 17 numbers used. You are given one word to start you off, so you can begin by entering any letters from this word wherever they appear in the grid. Each word you make must be in good Latin (you can check the Latin to English word list at the end, if you need to). As you decode each letter, write it in the 'Letters deciphered' table and cross it off in the 'Letters used' table.

9 R	6 O	3 M	12 A	10 N	4 U	14 S	■	10
1	■	15	■	■	■	4	■	6
5	15	4	14	■	2	4	1	14
15	■	14	■	14	■	14	■	■
6	■	■	17	1	9	■	■	12
■	■	10	■	7	■	2	■	13
12	16	15	9	■	8	4	4	14
3	■	7	■	■	■	6	■	4
6	■	6	11	11	1	5	4	3

Letters deciphered:

1	2	3 M	4 U	5	6 O	7	8	9 R	10 N	11	12 A	13
14 S	15	16	17									

Letters used:

A	B	C	D	E	F̶	G	H̶	I	J̶	K̶	L̶	M
N	O	P	Q	R	S	T	U	V	W̶	X̶	Y̶	Z̶

23 A numbers game

See how many Roman numbers you can find in the grid below. They may be written across, down or even diagonally. They could also be written backwards!

UNUS	OCTO	QUINTUS
DUO	NOVEM	SEXTUS
TRES	DECEM	SEPTIMUS
QUATTUOR	PRIMUS	OCTAVUS
QUINQUE	SECUNDUS	NONUS
SEX	TERTIUS	DECIMUS
SEPTEM	QUARTUS	

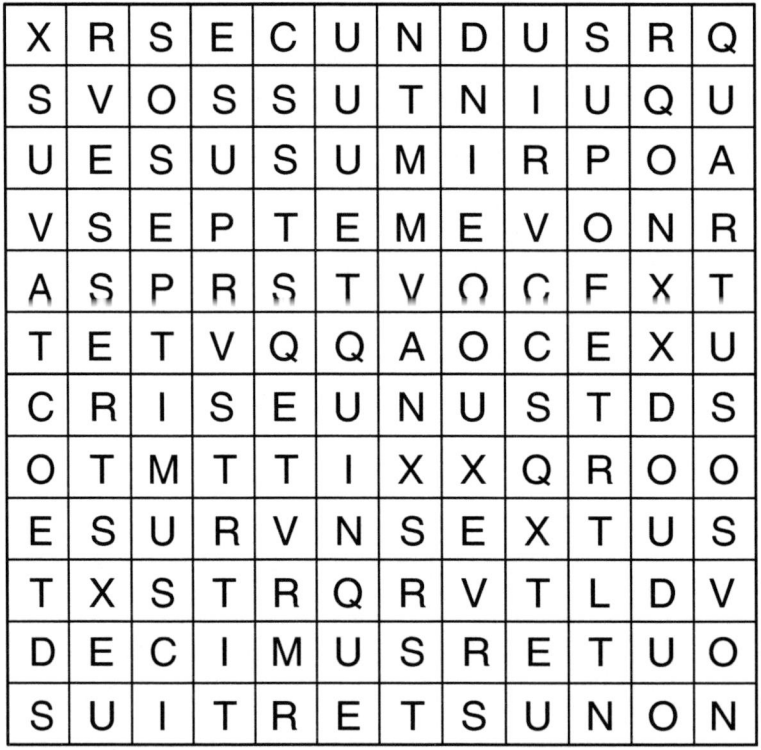

X	R	S	E	C	U	N	D	U	S	R	Q
S	V	O	S	S	U	T	N	I	U	Q	U
U	E	S	U	S	U	M	I	R	P	O	A
V	S	E	P	T	E	M	E	V	O	N	R
A	S	P	R	S	T	V	O	C	F	X	T
T	E	T	V	Q	Q	A	O	C	E	X	U
C	R	I	S	E	U	N	U	S	T	D	S
O	T	M	T	T	I	X	X	Q	R	O	O
E	S	U	R	V	N	S	E	X	T	U	S
T	X	S	T	R	Q	R	V	T	L	D	V
D	E	C	I	M	U	S	R	E	T	U	O
S	U	I	T	R	E	T	S	U	N	O	N

24 Sudoku

You probably know how Sudoku works. All you have to do is to place numbers one to nine in each vertical and horizontal line, and make sure that each number appears only once in each of the nine 3x3 squares. The difference here is that this is Roman Sudoku! Use the Roman numbers as below.

Roman numbers:

1	2	3	4	5	6	7	8	9
I	II	III	IV	V	VI	VII	VIII	IX

Good luck – feliciter!

VII		VI		II			I	
	I			III		V		
	IV			VII		II	VIII	VI
			VIII	VII		III		
VI				IX				IV
	IX		IV	VI				
V	III	VIII		I			IX	
		I		V			VII	
	II			IV		I		V

25 Cryptic Latin crossword

In this crossword, the clues are hidden in cryptic English but the answers must be in Latin! If you need help, you can use the word lists at the back of the book.

ACROSS

2   My shout (5)
4   Clear as mud in my presence (5)
6   Blowing fuses makes you tired in the South (6)
8   Fun use of one inside (4)
10 Not just you! (2,3)
11 OK to be buzzy outside the North (4)
12 Sounds like it was in the drink but came out again (2,4)
14 Destroy when eel breaks up the party? (5)
15 Across the moving North star (4)

DOWN

1   Your drink taken from safe? (4)
3   Walk with a disoderly mob moving about as you learn shorthand (6)
5   What is a pound with an 'o' but no 'i'? (4)
7   Learner's left asleep, all too often (5)
9   A number with rest disturbed (4)
10 Rerate mixture from the land (1,5)
13 Rage about on the farm (4)

26 Mini crossword

In this crossword, the clues are in Latin but the answers are in English. If you need help, you can use the Latin to English word list at the back of the book.

ACROSS
4   irae (2,5)
5   sunt (3)
6   sed (3)
8   auxilio (3,4)

DOWN
1   sagittae (2,5)
2   et (3)
3   aedificamus (2,5)
7   quis (3)

Note: Where a verb is given as a clue, such as maneo (= I remain), the word 'I' will sometimes, but not always, appear in the answer.

27 Mini Latin crossword

In this crossword, the clues are in English but the answers are in Latin. If you need help, you can use the English to Latin word list at the back of the book.

ACROSS
1   Thus (3)
4   Well (4)
5   Daughter (5)
6   You (sing., acc.) (2)
8   For a long time (3)
9   Man (3)

DOWN
1   I am (3)
2   Down from (2)
3   But (3)
4   Wars (nom.) (5)
5   I made (4)
7   Through (3)

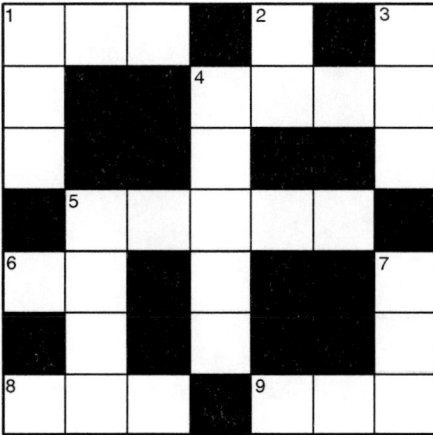

28 The emperor

Fill in the words in Latin going across and then you can read the word which goes down through the middle of the grid to discover a Roman emperor. Use the English to Latin word list at the back for help, if you need to.

CLUES
1   He was killing (7)
2   Clear (6)
3   She was present (6)
4   Known (5)
5   Sword (7)
6   Master (7)
7   God (4)
8   He ordered (6)

The emperor is: __ __ __ __ __ __ __

29 The cause of the trouble?

Fill in the grid below to discover a well known troublemaker in the ancient world. Put together the letters from the shaded boxes and see if you can make a name from the letters. Use the English to Latin word list at the back, if you need help.

ACROSS

1	She is present (5)
4	I entered (7)
9	They have put (9)
10	To (2)
12	Down from (2)
13	Well (4)
14	Love! (sing.) (3)
15	You (sing.) hold (5)
18	I have been away (4)
19	You (sing.) give (3)
21	Our women (7)

24	I loved (5)
25	You are away (4)
26	There (3)
27	Now (3)
28	Safe men (nom.) (4)
29	Thus (3)
30	He has walked (9)

DOWN

2	You (sing.) were destroying (7)
3	She overcomes (7)

5	At last (6)
6	Street (3)
7	It is (3)
8	Tired men (acc.) (6)
11	You (sing.) sleep (6)
16	Of messengers (9)
17	From fields (5)
18	They were present (7)
20	Immediately (6)
22	Of the slave (5)
23	I watch (6)
24	Friends (5)

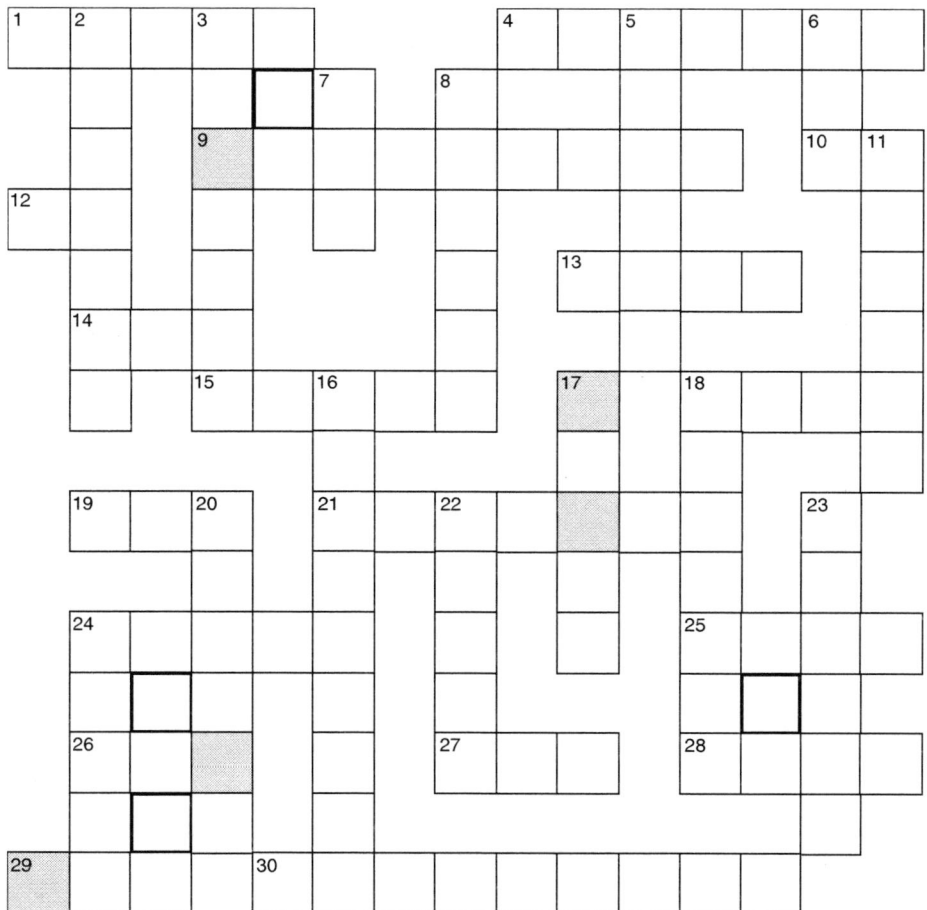

The troublemaker is: __ __ __ __ __

30 They were all there

In this crossword, all but one of the answers have been taken out and printed below. Your job is to fit all the other words back into the grid, and then write the clues! Don't forget to write the length of the answer in brackets.

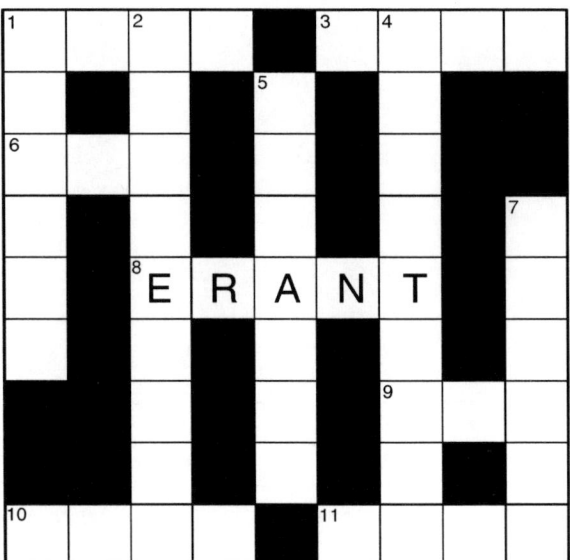

NOS
VIR

ESNE
NOTA
STAS
TUIS

ERANT

ABERAS
TANDEM

UNDARUM

IUSSERUNT
SPECTAVIT

ACROSS

1 _____

3 _____

6 _____

8 They were (5)

9 _____

10 _____

11 _____

DOWN

1 _____

2 _____

4 _____

5 _____

7 _____

31 Mums

In the table below, six mythological mothers have been separated from their famous children. Your job is to reunite them all, by reading the clues and putting the names into the boxes.

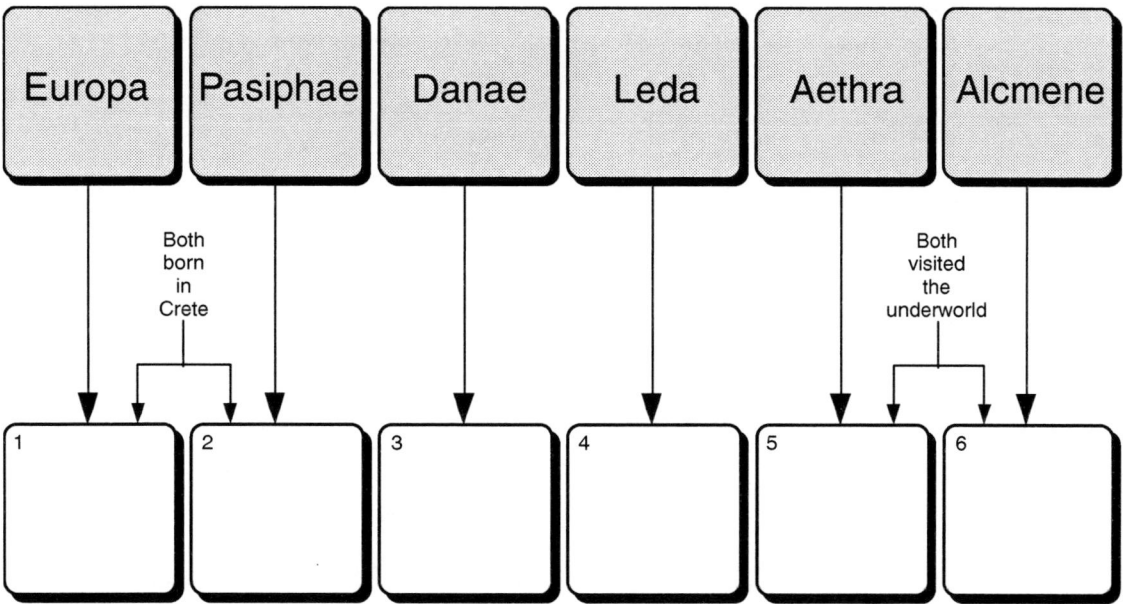

The children

1   Famous king of Crete, son of Zeus.
2   Horrible monster, half man, half bull.
3   Slayer of the gorgon.
4   Lady whose great beauty caused the Trojan War.
5   King of Athens who killed number 2.
6   Son of Jupiter who performed 12 labours.

32 Crossword

In this crossword, the clues are in Latin but the answers are all in English. If you need help, you can use the Latin to English word list at the back of the book.

ACROSS
6   amamus reginam (2,4,6)
7   prope (4)
8   audi (4)
9   turba (5)
10   viris (2,3)
12   quinque (4)
14   cum (4)
15   faciebamus (2,4,5)

DOWN
1   timemus vina (2,4,5)
2   quattuor (4)
3   currimus (2,3)
4   multum (4)
5   consumebat (2,3,6)
11   videmus (2,3)
13   etiam (4)
14   quem (4)

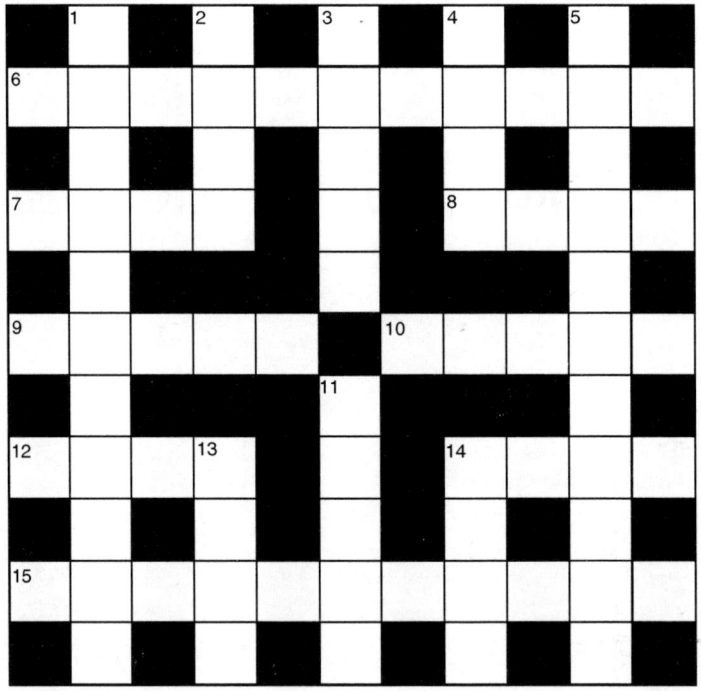

33 Latin crossword

In this crossword, the clues are in English but the answers are all in Latin. If you need help, you can use the English to Latin word list at the back of the book.

ACROSS

1   Girl (6)
2   Eight (4)
5   I was (4)
7   She fights (6)
10 I loved (5)
12 He has been away (5)
14 For sailors (6)
15 Ask! (sing.) (4)
16 Tall lady (nom.) (4)
17 Wind (6)

DOWN

1   Boys (nom.) (5)
3   I decide (9)
4   We led (7)
6   They have loved (9)
8   Your things (3)
9   She has prepared (7)
11 Not (3)
13 Across (5)

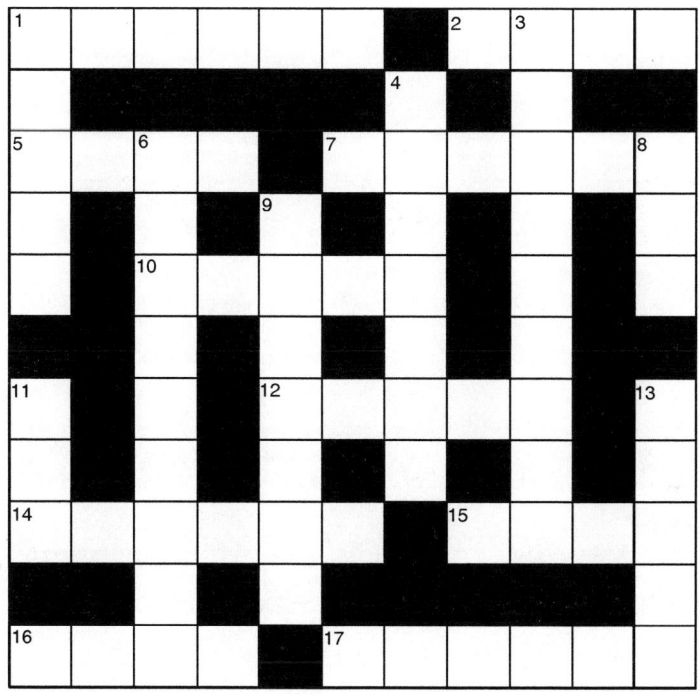

34 Crossword

In this crossword, the clues are in Latin but the answers are all in English. If you need help, you can use the Latin to English word list at the back of the book.

ACROSS

3   a te (2,3)
5   ride (5)
8   sed duo (3,3)
9   miser (4)
10   prope (4)
11   legimus (2,4)
12   est filius (2,3)
13   videmus (2,3)

DOWN

1   sagittae (3,3,5)
2   laetus agricola (5,6)
4   tui poetae (4,5)
6   bonus locus (9)
7   oppido (3,4)

Note: Where a verb is given as a clue, such as maneo (= I remain), the pronoun will sometimes, but not always, appear in the answer.

35 British tribes and towns

Find the tribes and towns in the grid below. They may be written across, down, diagonally or they could be written backwards! If you want to see what these towns are called today, see the solution on page 55.

AQUAE SULIS
ATREBATES
BRIGANTES
CALLEVA
CAMULODUNUM
CORINIUM
DEVA

DUBRIS
DUROTRIGES
EBORACUM
GLEVUM
ISCA
LINDUM
LONDINIUM

ORDOVICES
PARISI
REGNENSES
SILURES
VERULAMIUM
VINDOLANDA

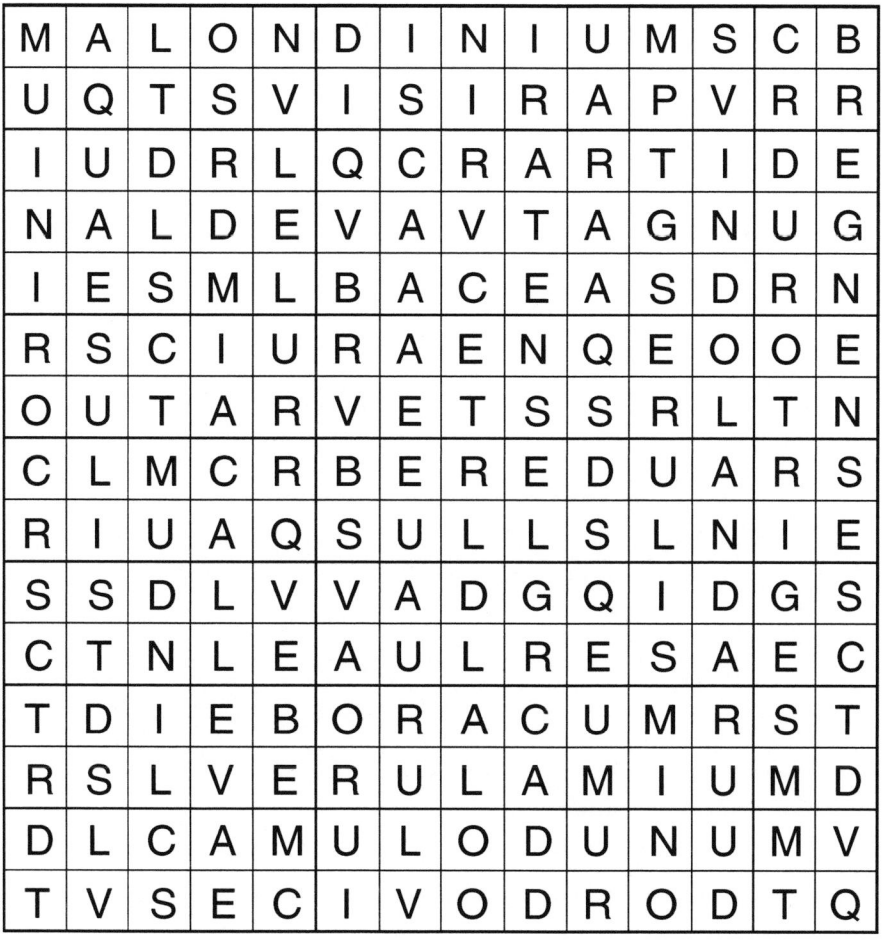

M	A	L	O	N	D	I	N	I	U	M	S	C	B
U	Q	T	S	V	I	S	I	R	A	P	V	R	R
I	U	D	R	L	Q	C	R	A	R	T	I	D	E
N	A	L	D	E	V	A	V	T	A	G	N	U	G
I	E	S	M	L	B	A	C	E	A	S	D	R	N
R	S	C	I	U	R	A	E	N	Q	E	O	O	E
O	U	T	A	R	V	E	T	S	S	R	L	T	N
C	L	M	C	R	B	E	R	E	D	U	A	R	S
R	I	U	A	Q	S	U	L	L	S	L	N	I	E
S	S	D	L	V	V	A	D	G	Q	I	D	G	S
C	T	N	L	E	A	U	L	R	E	S	A	E	C
T	D	I	E	B	O	R	A	C	U	M	R	S	T
R	S	L	V	E	R	U	L	A	M	I	U	M	D
D	L	C	A	M	U	L	O	D	U	N	U	M	V
T	V	S	E	C	I	V	O	D	R	O	D	T	Q

36 Cryptic Latin crossword

The answers to this brain-teaser are all in Latin. You may need to use the word lists at the back for help.

ACROSS

1   A point in my mother, my man (4)
2   King in mix up for Santa – it's quite clear! (6)
5   Sounds like a sighting around the coast with seven others (7)
8   Male sheep not pleased at all to meet me! (4)
11 Nab a top pug reformed at pole before they began to attack (11)
12 A street object (4)
15 It's a German car you're hearing (7)
17 You were there, around as dear (6)
18 In best bib or tucker for me sipping (4)

DOWN

1   It's me or him inside, for my man (3)
3   I played around American 51st state (4)
4   It's their problem in suicide (3)
6   Limp set around in religious buildings (7)
7   A bar tap confused was preparing (7)
9   Five operating systems mark you out (3)
10 Don't sit about! (3)
13 A learner takes a grand back – she's a bad girl (4)
14 8 Across loses a grand – that makes me so mad (3)
16 I stand about in store (3)

37 By Jupiter!

All these characters were children of Jupiter. See if you can discover how they might have called him, when you can read the word which goes down through the middle of the grid.

CLUES

1   Brother of Pollux, one of the two Dioscuri (6)
2   Wife of Menelaus, taken by Paris to Troy (5)
3   Wearer of lionskin, performer of 12 Labours (8)
4   King of Crete, father of Ariadne (5)
5   Goddess of hunting and archery (5)
6   Helmet wearing goddess of wisdom (7)
7   Killer of Medusa (7)
8   Messenger with invisibility cap and winged sandals (7)
9   God of war, father of Romulus (4)

Jupiter's name: __ __ __ __ __ __ __ __ __

38 Scared?

In the table below, the words have been taken out and printed below, all except for the word timeo (= I fear). Your job is to fit all the other words back into the grid.

5 letters	11 letters
ABSUM	AGRICOLARUM
ADSUM	AQUAS AMAVIT
ALTAM	DORMIVERUNT
AMAVI	SCRIBO AD VOS
AUDIS	
IN IRA	
IN MEA	
IRATA	
IUBEO	
MISIT	
MULTI	
SACRA	
SAEVA	
STANT	
~~TIMEO~~	
TUTUM	

39 I've been there

Look carefully at the grid below. The object of the puzzle is to find out which letter of the alphabet is represented by each of the 16 numbers used. You are given one word to start you off, so you can begin by entering any letters from this word wherever they appear in the grid. Each word you make must be in good Latin (you can check the Latin to English word list at the back if you need to). As you decode each letter, write it in the 'Letters deciphered' table and cross it off in the 'Letters used' table.

	8	12	4	1	12	9	2	
4	■			5	■	■	■	4
5	■	12 A	6	15	2	14	■	11
8	■	3 D	■	15	■	8	■	14
12	3	10 F	7	5	15	7	4	1
13	■	7 U	■	13	■	1	■	15
12	■	2 I	15	12	1	12	■	11
1	■	■	■	4	■	■	■	14
■	9	5	14	1	15	7	16	■

Letters deciphered:

1	2	3	4	5	6	7	8	9	10	11	12	13
	I	D				U			F		A	
14	15	16										

Letters used:

A	B	C	D	E	F	G	H̶	I	J̶	K̶	L̶	M
N	O	P̶	Q̶	R	S	T	U	V	W̶	X	Y̶	Z̶

40 Latin crossword

In this crossword, the clues are in English but the answers are all in Latin. If you need help, you can use the English to Latin word list at the back of the book.

ACROSS
2   Bad woman (4)
6   Field (4)
8   God (acc.) (4)
9   You (pl.) slept (11)
11 Across (5)
12 Near (5)
15 They were showing (11)
18 O bad man (4)
20 Safe things (4)
21 Fear! (4)

DOWN
1   For the field (4)
3   I loved (5)
4   To (2)
5   I have led (4)
7   Roman women (nom.) (7)
9   She gives (3)
10 He writes (7)
13 It is (3)
14 I am present (5)
16 You (sing.) stand (4)
17 Of a known man (4)
19 And (2)

41 A fighting force

Fill in the grid below to uncover a fighting force in Rome. Put together the letters from the shaded boxes and see if you can make the name of this force from the letters. Use the English to Latin word list at the back, if you need help.

ACROSS

1	They have put (9)
5	However (5)
9	Swords (acc.) (7)
11	He laughed (5)
12	Angry man (nom.) (6)
14	For the safe men (5)
15	Hold! (4)
19	To (2)
20	Three (4)
22	Slave (nom.) (6)
24	Order! (4)
26	They were frightening (9)
29	I read (4)
30	Of a wretched man (6)
33	You (pl.) put (7)
34	Sacred woman (acc.) (6)

DOWN

2	Arrows (acc.) (8)
3	You (pl.) were (6)
4	Where (3)
6	She sent (5)
7	Of a known man (4)
8	The frightened men (acc.) (11)
10	Shields (5)
13	But (3)
16	And (2)
17	She is (3)
18	They are (4)
21	O Roman (6)
23	First men (acc.) (6)
25	By war (5)
27	Horses (acc.) (5)
28	Of the field (4)
31	Thus (3)
32	Now (3)

The fighting force was: __ __ __ __ __ __

42 Crossword

In this crossword, the clues are in Latin but the answers are all in English. If you need help, you can use the Latin to English word list at the back of the book.

ACROSS
4   tenet unum virum (5,3,3)
6   laboro (1,4)
7   habuimus (2,3)
9   sunt (3)
10   vir (3)
11   viri (3)
13   ibi (5)
14   oppida (5)
16   nostro poeta (4,3,4)

DOWN
1   aderas (3,4,4)
2   filius (3)
3   saeva ira (6,5)
5   etiam (4)
8   consume (3)
12   ab (4)
15   sed (3)

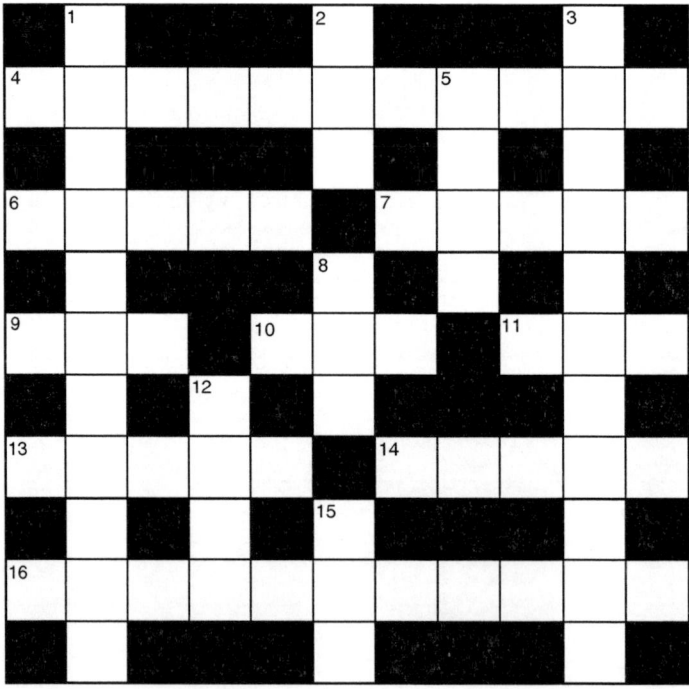

Note: Where a verb is given as a clue, such as maneo (= I remain), the pronoun will sometimes, but not always, appear in the answer.

43 Cryptic Latin crossword

The answers to this brain-teaser are all in Latin. You may need to use the word lists at the back for help.

ACROSS

3 Nor am I confused about empire builders (6)
6 Uses his ears (5)
7 Object when they are tired (6)
9 Anger about air (3)
11 No dog - why not? (3,3)
14 Respect a good look inside (6)
16 Through personal contents (3)
17 Irish gunmen go to the South and find angry men there (6)
19 Sounds like your wager - he's giving the orders (5)
20 Made an attempt while you were standing around (6)

DOWN

1 Boy's behaviour without the French (5)
2 Sounds like ages since I'd take you (3)
4 It sounds like they are not here (6)
5 19 across is past it (6)
8 And take note at well known lady (2,4)
10 I'll come out on top if I take professional to court out of order (6)
12 Confuse 101 so-so friends in war (6)
13 Ooo – you are awful, lady (2,4)
15 You destroy this mixed United football team (5)
18 Sounds like you'll go with me (3)

44 Following orders

The Roman army could be quite confusing because lots of different soldiers had to work together but, if you were a soldier, you had to know who they all were. See if you can discover which individual might be most important to you by reading the word which goes down through the middle of the grid.

N.B. Some of the solutions are in English, others are in Latin – just to keep you on your toes!

CLUES

1 A group of about 500 soldiers – one of ten in a unit (6)
2 This man was a guard commander (11)
3 This man was the standard bearer (8)
4 This man was the unit's commander (6)
5 This man was a young officer, often from a rich family (7)
6 This man blew the trumpet (8)
7 A unit of around 5000 soldiers (6)
8 This man was second in command of 80 men (5)
9 A group of around 80 soldiers (7)

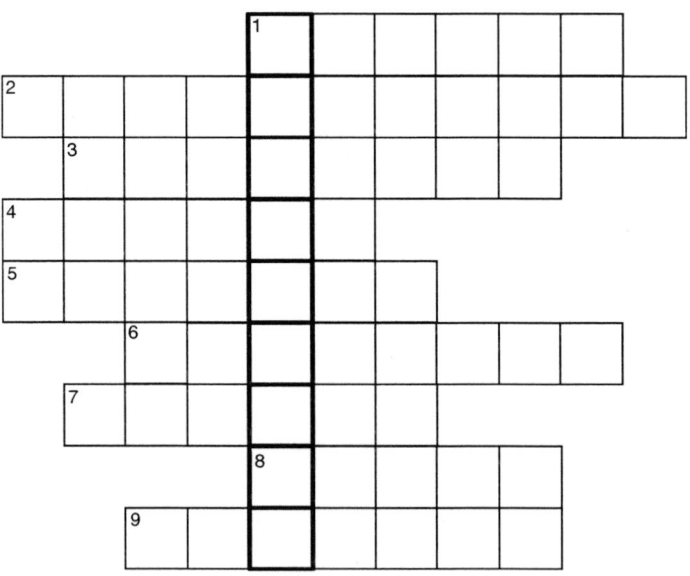

Your main man: __ __ __ __ __ __ __ __ __

45 Truly heroic

Solve the riddle by answering all the statements made below. As you answer each question, insert a letter in the grid below where you will see two words formed.

Word 1
1   My first is in hero but not in error.
2   My second is in sword and also in Rome.
3   My third is in river and also in run.
4   My fourth is in Athens and also in altar.
5   My fifth is in Tiber but not in bridge.
6   My sixth is in Capitol and also in Hill.
7   My seventh is in unus and but not in tres.
8   My eighth is in senate but not in parliament.

Word 2
1   My first is in Cumae and also in Cupid.
2   My second is in amo and also in love.
3   My third is in Clusium but not in Porsenna.
4   My fourth is in Lucretius but not in Etruscan.
5   My fifth is in armed but not in army.
6   My sixth is in sex and also in six.

My whole is a hero of early Rome.

1	2	3	4	5	6	7	8

1	2	3	4	5	6

46 Crossword

In this crossword, the clues are in Latin but the answers are all in English. If you need help, you can use the Latin to English word list at the back of the book.

ACROSS
1 nos decem (2,3)
3 sed iam (3,3)
6 vide (3)
7 ab ira (4,5)
8 sum? (2,1)
12 verbum (4)
13 roga me (3,2)
14 aqua (5)
15 specta (5)
16 cum (4)

18 vos (3)
21 in meo loco (2,2,5)
22 et (3)
23 etiam meum (4,2)
24 ibi (5)

DOWN
1 ostendimus (2,4)
2 scribunt (4,5)
3 a me (2,2)
4 regimus (2,4)

5 ab (4)
9 maneo (1,4)
10 bellum (3)
11 caelum est tutum (3,2,4)
14 cur (3)
15 damus (3,4)
17 tenuit me (4,2)
19 olim (4)
20 ludete (4)

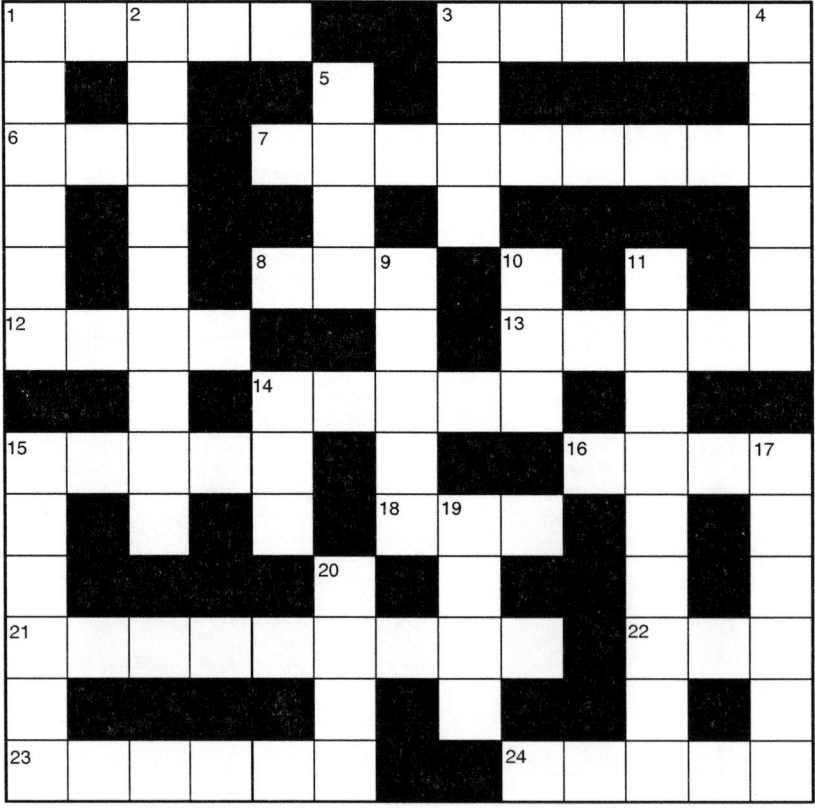

Note: Where a verb is given as a clue, such as maneo (= I remain), the pronoun will sometimes, but not always, appear in the answer.

47 A place in the camp

A Roman camp was usually very well organised, with a place for everyone and everything. See if you can find all the words mentioned in the grid below. They may be written across, down, diagonally or they could also be written backwards! Good luck.

CAMP
CENTURION
DAGGER
EAGLE
GATEHOUSE
GRANARY
GUARD

HEADQUARTERS
HELMET
HOSPITAL
LATRINE
LEGATE
OPTIO
PRAETORIUM

PRINCIPIA
SIGNIFER
SPEAR
SOLDIER
SWORD
TESSERARIUS
TRIBUNE

G	A	T	E	H	O	U	S	E	M	R	M
R	S	T	R	S	S	W	O	R	D	T	U
H	O	L	H	E	U	D	R	A	U	G	I
E	N	L	E	S	I	G	N	I	F	E	R
A	O	P	A	G	R	D	O	I	T	P	O
D	I	R	R	T	A	T	L	H	T	Y	T
Q	R	I	E	R	R	T	M	O	O	R	E
U	U	N	G	O	E	I	E	M	S	A	A
A	T	C	G	O	S	N	N	S	L	N	R
R	N	I	A	M	S	E	U	E	L	A	P
T	E	P	D	P	E	L	L	B	O	R	M
E	C	I	E	H	T	O	L	G	I	G	A
R	L	A	T	I	P	S	O	H	A	R	C
S	R	T	M	S	R	H	E	L	M	E	T

48 Crossword

In this crossword, the clues are in Latin but the answers are all in English. If you need help, you can use the Latin to English word list at the back of the book.

ACROSS
7   dixit (2,4)
8   ostendit (6)
9   necavit (6)
10 novi viri (3,3)
11 ducite nos (4,2)
13 via (6)
14 vino (2,4)
17 novus puer (3,3)
20 noster vir (3,3)
22 proelium (6)
23 manete (6)
24 See 6 Down (6)

DOWN
1   habitamus (2,4)
2   vocavit (6)
3   feci (1,3)
4   est in (2,2)
5   bello (3,3)
6   faciebamus (2,4,6)
    Also 24 Across
12 vide (3)
13 filius (3)
15 vos viri (3,3)
16 sum malus (1,2,3)
18 capimus (6)
19 terrae (2,4)
21 novem (4)
22 a me (2,2)

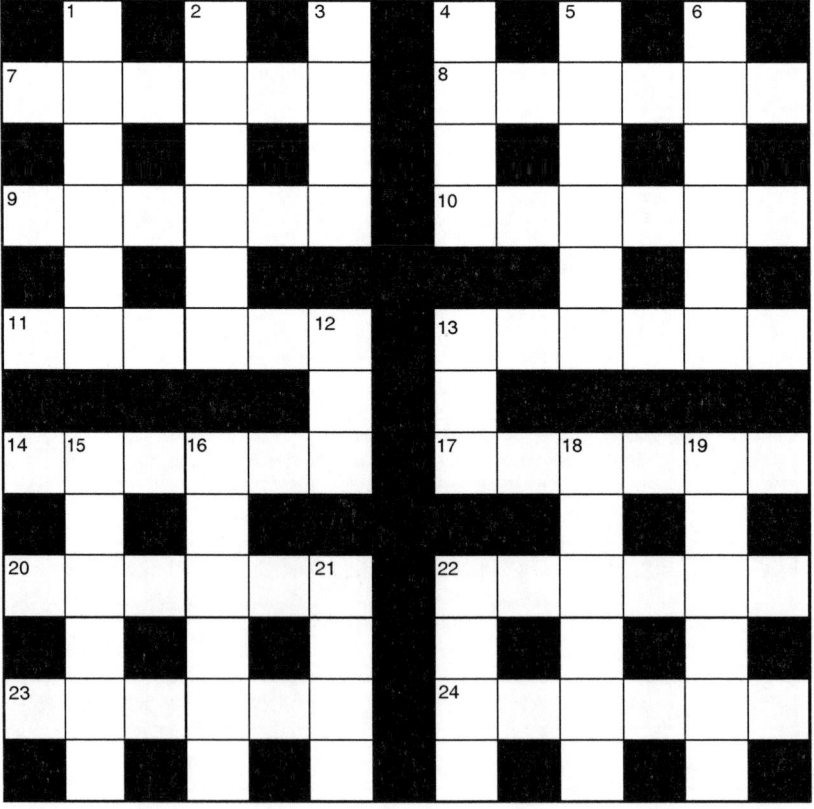

Note: Where a verb is given as a clue, such as maneo (= I remain), the pronoun will sometimes, but not always, appear in the answer.

49 Latin crossword

In this crossword, the clues are in English but the answers are all in Latin. If you need help, you can use the English to Latin word list at the back of the book.

ACROSS
1   Inhabitant (6)
4   He was giving (5)
7   I love (3)
9   You (sing.) drink (5)
10 One thing (4)
12 I have been (3)
13 She loves (4)
15 I am (3)
16 Thus (3)
17 My men (nom.) (3)
18 Now (3)
21 There (3)
22 You (sing.) love (4)

24 Six (3)
28 By a safe thing (4)
29 Praise! (5)
30 For a long time (3)
31 Savage things (5)
32 They call (6)

DOWN
1   She orders (5)
2   Of food (4)
3   I played (4)
4   I give (2)
5   A good thing (5)
6   Fear! (pl.) (6)

8   I sent myself (2,4)
11 You (sing.) say (5)
13 To a friend (5)
14 You are (2)
17 Of a wretched man (6)
19 Me (2)
20 You sing (6)
23 Tall women (nom.) (5)
25 They were (5)
26 By a high thing (4)
27 Safe things (4)
30 Give! (sing.) (2)

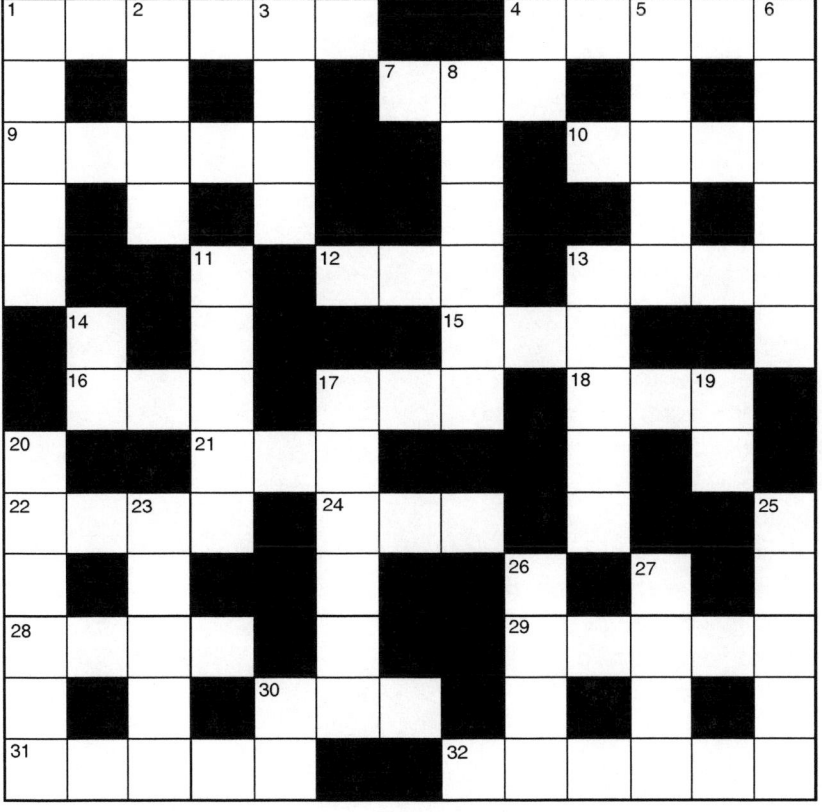

50 Cryptic Latin crossword

The answers to this terrible torture are all in Latin. If you need help, you can use the word lists at the back of the book.

ACROSS

1	He is obviously as cruel without East (6)
4	A quiet confusion, therefore (6)
6	Take rum after the metallic sign of gleaming metal (5)
9	Tided around as a gift (5)
11	Foodstuffs for two citizens' band users (4)
12	No room for learner in a stall for the high ups (5)
13	I stand the cost, after the first hundred (3)
14	Safe and sound in fancy dresses (5)
15	Mixed duties set out for a long time (3)
17	Take the train in Birmingham? (3,4)
19	Look again in t'cave for a former killing (7)
22	Their girl confused about America (3)
24	Quadruped queues but not East (5)
26	All south – not likely (3)
27	Lots of people seen in headgear (5)
28	Out of Latin air confused makes these bouts of rage (4)
29	Object of Neptune's surroundings (5)
32	In descant or tune? (5)
33	Member of Parliament always in the eye (6)
34	You love it, if it's a rug (6)

DOWN

1	I took nice pig inside (4)
2	Sounds like the governor's from farming stock (8)
3	I carried a six pack to the harbour (7)
5	What – only a pound? (4)
7	Inside you rest as you are standing (4)
8	A bun or a cake from one man (2,3)
9	He is a tad relaxed about giving (3)
10	You are the only girl for me (2,3)
15	Sad reflection on your gift (3)
16	United Nations on top of one woman (3)
18	Tar sounds like a ne'er do well (5)
20	Shortened rugby game upset among first half of crowds – I'd run (5)
21	They came on venture north (8)
23	Surfer's only chance! (3,4)
24	Tear was rolling (4)
25	I am counting (3)
30	One thing is an object (4)
31	Be as upset as you like – you're not here (4)

Solutions

1   Mini crossword

ACROSS		DOWN	
4	I show	1	I see
5	Seventh	2	However
7	Never	3	High
		5	Sail
		6	Then

2   Mini Latin crossword

ACROSS		DOWN	
4	Romanus	1	do
5	ancilla	2	sagitta
6	festino	3	tu
		7	et
		8	ne

3   A top man

1. rego
2. octo
3. meus
4. unda
5. ludo
6. unus
7. suus

Romulus was the first of the seven kings of Rome.

4   Keep smiling

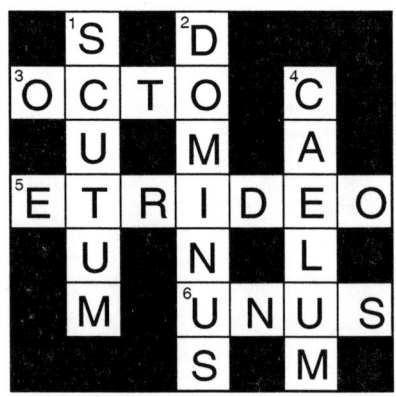

ACROSS		DOWN	
3	Eight (4)	1	Shield (6)
5	And I laugh (2,5)	2	Master (7)
6	One (4)	4	Sky (6)

5   Why not?

Letters deciphered:

1 C	2 S	3 A	4 N	5 U	6 D	7 I	8 O	9 T	10 M	11 R	12 E	13 V
14 X	15 B											

6   At home

```
C M U I L Y T S I R E P P
O U L R O I D F S B A T
M S L A T R D U A F L F
P R F B T I S U I L R
L A I N L S I N L I S
U I T I I A T B A I V U
V P M R H A T R I U M M
I M A P I O R L T S O
U O I T L C R E D I T D
M D R L E U L T T P F A
D P T R I R V I U A B I
S E C U A F D I N S M L
M A G I S T E R U I R I
F T I P T Y N I U M U F
T A B L I N U M I D S M
```

7   Sudoku

II	V	VI	IV	III	VIII	I	IX	VII
VII	VIII	III	IX	I	V	VI	IV	II
IX	I	IV	VI	VII	II	VIII	V	III
IV	III	I	VIII	II	VI	V	VII	IX
V	II	VII	III	IX	I	IV	VI	VIII
VIII	VI	IX	V	IV	VII	III	II	I
I	IX	V	II	VI	III	VII	VIII	IV
III	IV	VIII	VII	V	IX	II	I	VI
VI	VII	II	I	VIII	IV	IX	III	V

8 Crossword

ACROSS		DOWN	
5	Beautiful	1	Ten
8	Word	2	Build
9	Soon	3	Six
13	Messenger	4	But
		6	Two
		7	One
		9	Stand
		10	See
		11	Ask
		12	New

9 Find the monster!

ACROSS		DOWN	
1	porto	2	ostendo
4	discedo	3	templum
9	magnopere	5	servus
10	ad	6	dea
12	de	7	ego
13	quis	8	socius
14	diu	11	deinde
15	murus	16	respondeo
18	quid	17	tutus
19	hic	18	quartus
21	sagitta	20	contra
24	canto	22	gladius
25	tres	23	iterum
26	per	24	cupio
27	ira		
28	suus		
29	non		
30	constituo		

The monster is the **Minotaur**, the half man, half bull creature, kept in the Labyrinth on Crete until he was killed by Theseus.

10 Latin crossword

ACROSS		DOWN	
1	Aqua	1	Ager
2	Quod	3	Dico
5	Equus	4	Pulcher
6	Discedo	7	Pono
9	Poeta	8	Lego
10	Octo		
11	Ludo		

11 Cryptic Latin crossword

ACROSS		DOWN	
1	iam	2	murus
3	rogat	3	rego
5	cur ego	4	tamen
6	nos	6	nonus
7	non	7	notus
9	igitur	8	ager
10	sacer		
11	sum		

12 Arrow word

I			V		C			D	O
R		F	I	L	I	A		E	
A	G	E	R		B				P
		M		P	U	E	R		E
U		I			S		E		R
N	O	N		M		A	G	R	I
D		A	Q	U	A		I		C
A			R		I	N		U
	V		C	U	R		A		L
V	I	N	U	M		A			U
	A		M		A	B	S	U	M

13 Room in the house

CLUES

1	fortiter
2	parvus
3	iacio
4	pecunia
5	validus
6	liber
7	moneo
8	patria
9	ventus
10	primus

The **triclinium** was the name for a Roman dining room.

14 Fit the words

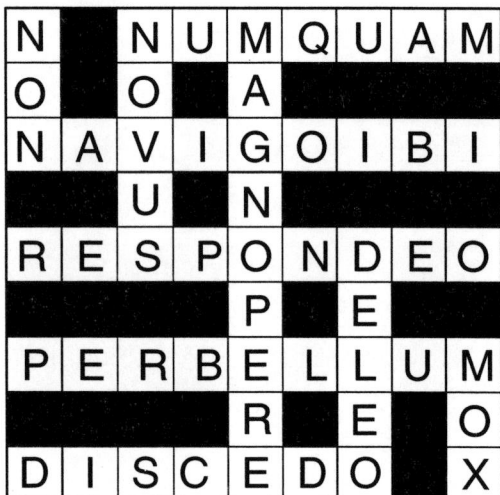

N		N	U	M	Q	U	A	M
O		O		A				
N	A	V	I	G	O	I	B	I
		U		N				
R	E	S	P	O	N	D	E	O
				P		E		
P	E	R	B	E	L	L	U	M
				R		E		O
D	I	S	C	E	D	O		X

15 Latin crossword

ACROSS
3 agricola
5 ad
6 sex
7 meus
8 de
9 ex
10 octo
11 amo
13 in
15 proelium

DOWN
1 tres
2 nos
3 aedifico
4 auxilium
7 mox
8 duo
12 olim
14 vos

16 Crossword

ACROSS
1 My master
5 Big
7 Field
8 We
9 Soon
10 Come
12 Then
13 Gold
14 My
15 Happy
16 Now
18 I destroy

DOWN
2 Am I
3 Suddenly
4 Second
6 Good
8 Wretched
9 Sleeps
11 Town
17 Out

17 Missing mythology

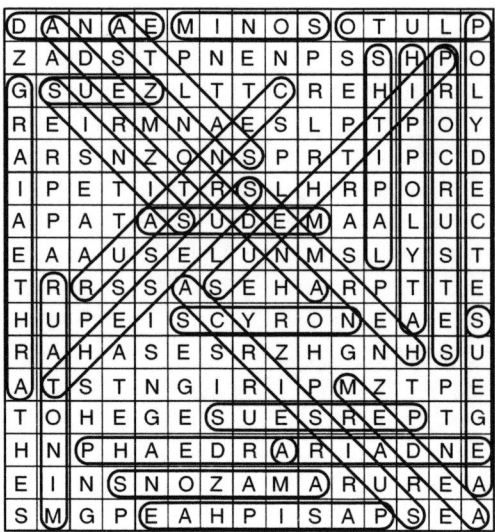

18 Mini crossword

ACROSS
1 I praise
4 Comes
6 Never
7 Seventh

DOWN
2 Roman
3 Enter
4 Calls
5 Seven

19 Mini Latin crossword

ACROSS
1 octavus
3 amicus
4 multus
5 Romanus

DOWN
2 ancilla

20 Good what?

1 magnopere
2 moveo
3 hasta
4 tandem
5 turba
6 regina
7 insula
8 saepe

nota bene means 'take good note' in English. It is normally just written as 'NB'.

21 Where and why?

ACROSS
1	I prepare (4)
5	I sing (5)
6	I rule (4)
9	There (3)
12	Well (4)
14	I am present (5)
15	I call (4)

DOWN
1	Through (3)
2	I ask (4)
3	Now (3)
4	Even (5)
7	Where? (3)
8	I praise (5)
10	I kill (4)
11	Why? (3)
13	I (3)

22 A Roman mystery

Letters deciphered:

1	2	3	4	5	6	7	8	9	10	11	12	13
I	Q	M	U	D	O	C	T	R	N	P	A	B

14	15	16	17									
S	E	G	V									

23 A numbers game

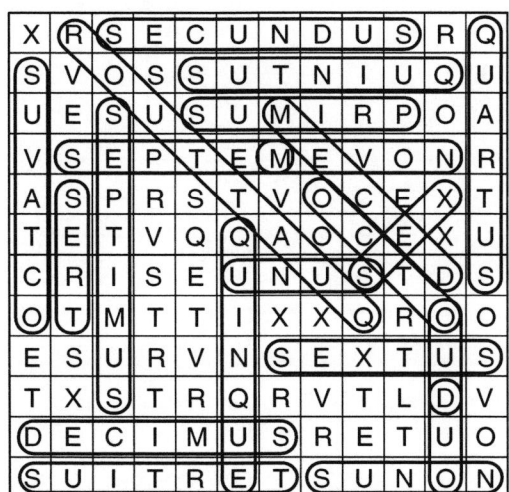

N.B. 'duo' can be circled in both directions.

24 Sudoku

VII	VIII	VI	V	II	IV	IX	I	III
II	I	IX	VI	III	VIII	V	IV	VII
III	IV	V	I	VII	IX	II	VIII	VI
I	V	IV	II	VIII	VII	VI	III	IX
VI	VII	II	III	IX	I	VIII	V	IV
VIII	IX	III	IV	VI	V	VII	II	I
V	III	VIII	VII	I	VI	IV	IX	II
IV	VI	I	IX	V	II	III	VII	VIII
IX	II	VII	VIII	IV	III	I	VI	V

25 Cryptic Latin crossword

ACROSS
2	clamo
4	adsum
6	fessus
8	unus
10	et ego
11	bene
12	ex aqua
14	deleo
15	trans

DOWN
1	tuus
3	ambulo
5	quod
7	saepe
9	tres
10	e terra
13	ager

26 Mini crossword

ACROSS
4	Of anger
5	Are
6	But
8	For help

DOWN
1	Of arrow
2	And
3	We build
7	Who

27 Mini Latin crossword

ACROSS
1	sic
4	bene
5	filia
6	te
8	diu
9	vir

DOWN
1	sum
2	de
3	sed
4	bella
5	feci
7	per

28　The emperor

1　necabat
2　clarus
3　aderat
4　notus
5　gladius
6　dominus
7　deus
8　iussit

Claudius became emperor of Rome in AD41 and remained in power until his death in AD54. His best known achievement was the occupation of Britain in AD43.

29　The cause of the trouble?

ACROSS		DOWN	
1	adest	2	delebas
4	intravi	3	superat
9	posuerunt	5	tandem
10	ad	6	via
12	de	7	est
13	bene	8	fessos
14	ama	11	dormis
15	tenes	16	nuntiorum
18	afui	17	agris
19	das	18	aderant
21	nostrae	20	statim
24	amavi	22	servi
25	abes	23	specto
26	ibi	24	amici
27	iam		
28	tuti		
29	sic		
30	ambulavit		

The cause of the trouble was **Paris**, who sneaked Helen of Sparta away and took her to Troy. This sequence of events led to the start of the Trojan War.

30　They were all there

ACROSS

1　For your men? (4)
3　Are you? (4)
6　We (3)
8　They were (5)
9　Man (3)
10　Well-known lady (4)
11　You (sing.) stand (4)

DOWN

1　At last (6)
2　They ordered (9)
4　He/she watched (9)
5　Of the waves (7)
7　You (sing.) were absent (6)

31　Mums

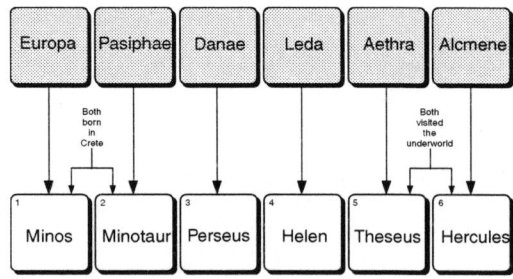

32　Crossword

ACROSS

6　We love queen
7　Near
8　Hear
9　Crowd
10　To men
12　Five
14　With
15　We were doing

DOWN

1　We fear wines
2　Four
3　We run
4　Much
5　He was eating
11　We see
13　Even
14　Whom

33 Latin crossword

ACROSS		DOWN	
1	puella	1	pueri
2	octo	3	constituo
5	eram	4	duximus
7	pugnat	6	amaverunt
10	amavi	8	tua
12	afuit	9	paravit
14	nautis	11	non
15	roga	13	trans
16	alta		
17	ventus		

34 Crossword

ACROSS		DOWN	
3	By you	1	For the arrow
5	Laugh	2	Happy farmer
8	But two	4	Your poets
9	Poor	6	Good place
10	Near	7	For town
11	We read		
12	Is son		
13	We see		

35 British tribes and towns

Roman names	Modern names
Aquae Sulis	Bath
Calleva	Silchester
Camulodunum	Colchester
Corinium	Cirencester
Deva	Chester
Dubris	Dover
Eboracum	York
Glevum	Gloucester
Isca	Exeter
Lindum	Lincoln
Londinium	London
Verulamium	St Albans
Vindolanda	Vindolanda

36 Cryptic Latin crossword

ACROSS		DOWN	
1	meum	1	meo
2	clarus	3	lusi
5	octavus	4	sui
8	iram	6	templis
11	oppugnabant	7	parabat
12	viam	9	vos
15	auditis	10	sta
17	aderas	13	mala
18	bibo	14	ira
		16	sto

37 By Jupiter!

1 Castor
2 Helen
3 Hercules
4 Minos
5 Diana
6 Minerva
7 Perseus
8 Mercury
9 Mars

Jupiter was often called the **thunderer** because, as king of the gods, he often threw thunderbolts at people when he was angry.

38 Scared?

39 I've been there

Letters deciphered:

1	2	3	4	5	6	7	8	9	10	11	12	13
T	I	D	N	E	G	U	C	V	F	O	A	B

14	15	16										
S	R	M										

40   Latin crossword

ACROSS		DOWN	
2	mala	1	agro
6	ager	3	amavi
8	deum	4	ad
9	dormivistis	5	duxi
11	trans	7	Romanae
12	prope	9	dat
15	ostendebant	10	scribit
18	male	13	est
20	tuta	14	adsum
21	time	16	stas
		17	noti
		19	et

41   A fighting force

ACROSS		DOWN	
1	posuerunt	2	sagittas
5	tamen	3	eratis
9	gladios	4	ubi
11	risit	6	misit
12	iratus	7	noti
14	tutis	8	perterritos
15	tene	10	scuta
19	ad	13	sed
20	tres	16	et
22	servus	17	est
24	iube	18	sunt
26	terrebant	21	Romane
29	lego	23	primos
30	miseri	25	bello
33	ponitis	27	equos
34	sacram	28	agri
		31	sic
		32	iam

A **legion** was a fighting unit of between 5000 and 6000 soldiers.

42   Crossword

ACROSS		DOWN	
4	Holds one man	1	You were here
6	I work	2	Son
7	We had	3	Savage anger
9	Are	5	Even
10	Man	8	Eat
11	Men	12	From
13	There	15	But
14	Towns		
16	From our poet		

43   Cryptic Latin crossword

ACROSS		DOWN	
3	Romani	1	pueri
6	audit	2	diu
7	fessos	4	absunt
9	ira	5	iussit
11	cur non	8	et nota
14	specta	10	supero
16	per	12	socios
17	iratos	13	es mala
19	iubet	15	deles
20	stabas	18	cum

44   Following orders

1 cohort
2 tesserarius
3 signifer
4 legate
5 tribune
6 cornicen
7 legion
8 optio
9 century

A **centurion** was a leader of a century – a group of around 80 soldiers. He was one of the most important people in the legion for many soldiers.

45   Truly heroic

| ¹H | ²O | ³R | ⁴A | ⁵T | ⁶I | ⁷U | ⁸S | | ¹C | ²O | ³C | ⁴L | ⁵E | ⁶S |

Horatius Cocles was the hero who managed to fight off the Etruscans single handed while his friends broke down the bridge over the river Tiber.

46   Crossword

ACROSS		DOWN	
1	We ten	1	We show
3	But now	2	They write
6	See	3	By me
7	From anger	4	We rule
8	Am I	5	From
12	Word	9	I stay
13	Ask me	10	War
14	Water	11	Sky is safe
15	Watch	14	Why
16	With	15	We give
18	You	17	Held me
21	In my place	19	Once
22	And	20	Play
23	Even my		
24	There		

47 A place in the camp

```
G A T E H O U S E M R M
R S T R S W O R D T U
H O L H E U D R A U G I
E N L E S I G N I F E R
A O P A G R D O I T P O
D I R R T A T L H T Y T
Q R I E R R T M O O R E
U U N G O E I E M S A A
A T C G O S N N S L N R
R N I A M S E U E L A P
T E P D P E L L B O R M
E C I E H T O L G I G A
R L A T I P S O H A R C
S R T M S R H E L M E T
```

48 Crossword

ACROSS		DOWN	
7	He said	1	We live
8	Showed	2	Called
9	Killed	3	I did
10	New men	4	Is in
11	Lead us	5	For war
13	Street	6	We were
14	By wine	12	See
17	New boy	13	Son
20	Our man	15	You men
22	Battle	16	I am bad
23	Remain	18	We take
24	Making	19	Of land
		21	Nine
		22	By me

49 Latin crossword

ACROSS		DOWN	
1	incola	1	iubet
4	dabat	2	cibi
7	amo	3	lusi
9	bibis	4	do
10	unum	5	bonum
12	fui	6	timete
13	amat	8	me misi
15	sum	11	dicis
16	sic	13	amico
17	mei	14	es
18	iam	17	miseri
21	ibi	19	me
22	amas	20	cantas
24	sex	23	altae
28	tuto	25	erant
29	lauda	26	alto
30	diu	27	tuta
31	saeva	30	da
32	vocant		

50 Cryptic Latin crossword

ACROSS		DOWN	
1	clarus	1	cepi
4	itaque	2	agricola
6	aurum	3	portavi
9	dedit	5	quid
11	cibi	7	stas
12	altas	8	ab uno
13	sto	9	dat
14	tutus	10	es una
15	diu	15	das
17	via nova	16	una
19	necavit	18	nauta
22	sua	20	curro
24	equus	21	venerunt
26	non	23	una unda
27	turba	24	erat
28	irae	25	sum
29	aquam	30	unum
32	canto	31	abes
33	semper		
34	amatis		

Latin to English word list

a	from, by
ab	from, by
absum, abesse, afui	I am away
ad	to
adsum, adesse, adfui	I am present, am here
aedifico, aedificare, aedificavi, aedificatum	I build
ager, agri, m.	field
agricola, agricolae, m.	farmer
altus, alta, altum	high, tall
ambulo, ambulare, ambulavi, ambulatum	I walk
amicus, amici, m.	friend
amo, amare, amavi, amatum	I love
ancilla, ancillae, f.	maid-servant
aqua, aquae, f.	water
audio, audire, audivi, auditum	I hear
aurum, auri, n.	gold
auxilium, auxilium, n.	help
bellum, belli, n.	war
bene	well
bibo, bibere, bibi	I drink
bonus, bona, bonum	good
caelum, caeli, n.	sky
canto, cantare, cantavi, cantatum	I sing
capio, capere, cepi, captum	I take
cibus, cibi, m.	food
clamo, clamare, clamavi, clamatum	I shout
clarus, clara, clarum	clear
constituo, constituere, constitui, constitutum	I decide
consumo, consumere, consumpsi, consumptum	I eat
contra	against
cum	with
cupio, cupere, cupivi, cupitum	I desire
cur?	why?
curro, currere, cucurri, cursum	I run
de	down from
dea, deae, f.	goddess
decem	ten
decimus, decima, decimum	tenth
deinde	then
deleo, delere, delevi, deletum	I destroy
deus, dei, m.	god
dico, dicere, dixi, dictum	I say
discedo, discedere, discessi, discessum	I depart

diu	for a long time
do, dare, dedi, datum	I give
dominus, domini, m.	master
dormio, dormire, dormivi, dormitum	I sleep
dormit	sleeps
duco, ducere, duxi, ductum	I lead
duo	two
e	out of
ego	I
equus, equi, m.	horse
et	and
etiam	even
ex	out of
facio, facere, feci, factum	I make, do
femina, feminae, f.	woman
fessus, fessa, fessum	tired
festino, festinare, festinavi, festinatum	I hurry
filia, filiae, f.	daughter
filius, filii, m.	son
fortiter	bravely
gladius, gladii, m.	sword
habeo, habere, habui, habitum	I have
habito, habitare, habitavi, habitatum	I live
hasta, hastae, f.	spear
hic	here
iacio, iacere, ieci, iactum	I throw
iam	now
ibi	there
igitur	therefore
in	in
incola, incolae, m.	inhabitant
insula, insulae, f.	island
intro, intrare, intravi, intratum	I enter
ira, irae, f.	anger
iratus, irata, iratum	angry
itaque	and so
iterum	again
iubeo, iubere, iussi, iussum	I order
laboro, laborare, laboravi, laboratum	I work
laetus, laeta, laetum	happy
laudo, laudare, laudavi, laudatum	I praise
lego, legere, legi, lectum	I read
liber, libri, m.	book
locus, loci, m.	place
ludo, ludere, lusi, lusum	I play
magister, magistri, m.	master
magnopere	greatly
magnus, magna, magnum	big

malus, mala, malum	bad
maneo, manere, mansi, mansum	I remain, stay
me	me
meus, mea, meum	my
miser, misera, miserum	wretched, poor
mitto, mittere, misi, missum	I send
moneo, monere, monui, monitum	I warn
moveo, movere, movi, motum	I move
mox	soon
multus, multa, multum	much
murus, muri, m.	wall
nauta, nautae, m.	sailor
navigo, navigare, navigavi, navigatum	I sail
ne	question mark
neco, necare, necavi, necatum	I kill
non	not
nonus, nona, nonum	ninth
nos	we
noster, nostra, nostrum	our
notus, nota, notum	known
novem	nine
novus, nova, novum	new
numquam	never
nuntius, nuntii, m.	messenger
octavus, octava, octavum	eighth
octo	eight
olim	once
oppidum, oppidi, n.	town
oppugno, oppugnare, oppugnavi, oppugnatum	I attack
ostendo, ostendere, ostendi, ostensum	I show
paro, parare, paravi, paratum	I prepare
parvus, parva, parvum	small
patria, patriae, f.	native land
pecunia, pecuniae, f.	money
per	through
periculum, periculi, n.	danger
perterritus, perterrita, perterritum	frightened
poeta, poetae, m.	poet
pono, ponere, posui, positum	I put
porto, portare, portavi, portatum	I carry
primus, prima, primum	first
proelium, proelii, n.	battle
prope	near
puella, puellae, f.	girl
puer, pueri, m.	boy
pugno, pugnare, pugnavi, pugnatum	I fight
pulcher, pulchra, pulchrum	beautiful
quartus, quarta, quartum	fourth
quattuor	four
quid?	what?
quinque	five
quintus, quinta, quintum	fifth
quis	who
quod	because
regina, reginae, f.	queen
rego, regere, rexi, rectum	I rule
respondeo, respondere, respondi, responsum	I answer
rideo, ridere, risi, risum	I laugh
rogat	asks
rogo, rogare, rogavi, rogatum	I ask
Romanus, Romana, Romanum	Roman
sacer, sacra, sacrum	sacred
saepe	often
saevus, saeva, saevum	savage
sagitta, sagittae, f.	arrow
scribo, scribere, scripsi, scriptum	I write
scutum, scuti, n.	shield
secundus, secunda, secundum	second
sed	but
semper	always
septem	seven
septimus, septima, septimum	seventh
servus, servi, m.	slave
sex	six
sextus, sexta, sextum	sixth
sic	thus
socius, socii, m.	ally
specto, spectare, spectavi, spectatum	I watch
statim	immediately
sto, stare, steti, statum	I stand
subito	suddenly
sum, esse, fui	I am
supero, superare, superavi, superatum	I overcome
suus, sua, suum	his, her, its, their (own)
tamen	however
tandem	at last
templum, templi, n.	temple
teneo, tenere, tenui, tentum	I hold
terra, terrae, f.	land
terreo, terrere, terrui, territum	I frighten
tertius, tertia, tertium	third
timeo, timere, timui	I fear

trans	across
tres	three
tu	you (sing.)
turba, turbae, f.	crowd
tutus, tuta, tutum	safe
tuus, tua, tuum	your
ubi, ubi?	when, where?
unda, undae, f.	wave
unus, una, unum	one
validus, valida, validum	strong
venio, venire, veni, ventum	I come
venit	comes
ventus, venti, m.	wind
verbum, verbi, n.	word
vester, vestra, vestrum	your
via, viae, f.	street
video, videre, vidi, visum	I see
vinum, vini, n.	wine
vir, viri, m.	man
vocat	calls
voco, vocare, vocavi, vocatum	I call
vos	you (pl.)

English to Latin word list

Across	trans
Again	iterum
Against	contra
Ally	socius, socii, m.
Always	semper
I am	sum, esse, fui
I am away	absum, abesse, afui
I am present	adsum, adesse, adfui
And	et
And so	itaque
Anger	ira, irae, f.
Angry	iratus, irata, iratum
I answer	respondeo, respondere, respondi, responsum
Arrow	sagitta, sagittae, f.
I ask	rogo, rogare, rogavi, rogatum
Asks	rogat
At last	tandem
I attack	oppugno, oppugnare, oppugnavi, oppugnatum
Bad	malus, mala, malum
Battle	proelium, proelii, n.
Beautiful	pulcher, pulchra, pulchrum
Because	quod
Big	magnus, magna, magnum
Book	liber, libri, m.
Boy	puer, pueri, m.
Bravely	fortiter
I build	aedifico, aedificare, aedificavi, aedificatum
But	sed
By	a, ab
I call	voco, vocare, vocavi, vocatum
Calls	vocat
I carry	porto, portare, portavi, portatum
Clear	clarus, clara, clarum
I come	venio, venire, veni, ventum
Comes	venit
Crowd	turba, turbae, f.
Danger	periculum, periculi, n.
Daughter	filia, filiae, f.
I decide	constituo, constituere, constitui, constitutum
I depart	discedo, discedere, discessi, discessum
I desire	cupio, cupere, cupivi, cupitum
I destroy	deleo, delere, delevi, deletum
I do	facio, facere, feci, factum

Down from	de
I drink	bibo, bibere, bibi
I eat	consumo, consumere, consumpsi, consumptum
Eight	octo
Eighth	octavus, octava, octavum
I enter	intro, intrare, intravi, intratum
Even	etiam
Farmer	agricola, agricolae, m.
I fear	timeo, timere, timui
Field	ager, agri, m.
Fifth	quintus, quinta, quintum
I fight	pugno, pugnare, pugnavi, pugnatum
First	primus, prima, primum
Five	quinque
Food	cibus, cibi, m.
For a long time	diu
Four	quattuor
Fourth	quartus, quarta, quartum
Friend	amicus, amici, m.
I frighten	terreo, terrere, terrui, territum
Frightened	perterritus, perterrita, perterritum
From	a, ab
Girl	puella, puellae, f.
I give	do, dare, dedi, datum
God	deus, dei, m.
Goddess	dea, deae, f.
Gold	aurum, auri, n.
Good	bonus, bona, bonum
Greatly	magnopere
Happy	laetus, laeta, laetum
I have	habeo, habere, habui, habitum
I hear	audio, audire, audivi, auditum
Help	auxilium, auxilium, n.
Here	hic
High	altus, alta, altum
I hold	teneo, tenere, tenui, tentum
Horse	equus, equi, m.
However	tamen
I hurry	festino, festinare, festinavi, festinatum
I	ego
Immediately	statim
In	in
Inhabitant	incola, incolae, m.
Island	insula, insulae, f.
I kill	neco, necare, necavi, necatum
Known	notus, nota, notum
Land	terra, terrae, f.

I laugh	rideo, ridere, risi, risum
I lead	duco, ducere, duxi, ductum
I live	habito, habitare, habitavi, habitatum
I love	amo, amare, amavi, amatum
Maid-servant	ancilla, ancillae, f.
I make	facio, facere, feci, factum
Man	vir, viri, m.
Master	dominus, domini, m.
Master	magister, magistri, m.
Me	me
Messenger	nuntius, nuntii, m.
Money	pecunia, pecuniae, f.
I move	moveo, movere, movi, motum
Much	multus, multa, multum
My	meus, mea, meum
Native land	patria, patriae, f.
Near	prope
Never	numquam
New	novus, nova, novum
Nine	novem
Ninth	nonus, nona, nonum
Not	non
Now	iam
Often	saepe
Once	olim
One	unus, una, unum
I order	iubeo, iubere, iussi, iussum
Our	noster, nostra, nostrum
Out of	e, ex
I overcome	supero, superare, superavi, superatum
Place	locus, loci, m.
I play	ludo, ludere, lusi, lusum
Poet	poeta, poetae, m.
Poor	miser, misera, miserum
I praise	laudo, laudare, laudavi, laudatum
I prepare	paro, parare, paravi, paratum
I put	pono, ponere, posui, positum
Queen	regina, reginae, f.
Question mark	ne
I read	lego, legere, legi, lectum
I remain	maneo, manere, mansi, mansum
Roman	Romanus, Romana, Romanum
I rule	rego, regere, rexi, rectum
I run	curro, currere, cucurri, cursum
Sacred	sacer, sacra, sacrum
Safe	tutus, tuta, tutum
I sail	navigo, navigare, navigavi, navigatum

Sailor	nauta, nautae, m.	War	bellum, belli, n.
Savage	saevus, saeva, saevum	I warn	moneo, monere, monui, monitum
I say	dico, dicere, dixi, dictum	I watch	specto, spectare, spectavi, spectatum
Second	secundus, secunda, secundum	Water	aqua, aquae, f.
I see	video, videre, vidi, visum	Wave	unda, undae, f.
I send	mitto, mittere, misi, missum	We	nos
Seven	septem	Well	bene
Seventh	septimus, septima, septimum	What	quid
Shield	scutum, scuti, n.	When	ubi
I shout	clamo, clamare, clamavi, clamatum	Where?	ubi?
I show	ostendo, ostendere, ostendi, ostensum	Who?	quis?
I sing	canto, cantare, cantavi, cantatum	Why?	cur?
Six	sex	Wind	ventus, venti, m.
Sixth	sextus, sexta, sextum	Wine	vinum, vini, n.
Sky	caelum, caeli, n.	With	cum
Slave	servus, servi, m.	Woman	femina, feminae, f.
I sleep	dormio, dormire, dormivi, dormitum	Word	verbum, verbi, n.
Sleeps	dormit	I work	laboro, laborare, laboravi, laboratum
Small	parvus, parva, parvum	Wretched	miser, misera, miserum
Son	filius, filii, m.	I write	scribo, scribere, scripsi, scriptum
Soon	mox	You (pl.)	vos
Spear	hasta, hastae, f.	You (sing.)	tu
I stand	sto, stare, steti, statum	Your	tuus, tua, tuum
I stay	maneo, manere, mansi, mansum	Your	vester, vestra, vestrum
Street	via, viae, f.		
Strong	validus, valida, validum		
Suddenly	subito		
Sword	gladius, gladii, m.		
I take	capio, capere, cepi, captum		
Tall	altus, alta, altum		
Temple	templum, templi, n.		
Ten	decem		
Tenth	decimus, decima, decimum		
Their	suus, sua, suum		
Then	deinde		
There	ibi		
Therefore	igitur		
Third	tertius, tertia, tertium		
Three	tres		
Through	per		
I throw	iacio, iacere, ieci, iactum		
Thus	sic		
Tired	fessus, fessa, fessum		
To	ad		
Town	oppidum, oppidi, n.		
Two	duo		
I walk	ambulo, ambulare, ambulavi, ambulatum		
Wall	murus, muri, m.		